BRINGING PRAYER TO LIFE

Bringing Prayer to Life

A use of poetry to enrich and enliven prayer

George Tolley

Pentland Books
Durham · Edinburgh · Oxford

First published in 2001 by
Pentland Books
1 Hutton Close
South Church
Bishop Auckland
Durham

British Library Cataloguing in Publication Data.
A catalogue record for this book is available
from the British Library.

ISBN 1 85821 906 X

Typeset by George Wishart & Associates, Whitley Bay.
Printed and bound by Antony Rowe Ltd., Chippenham.

For Joan

Acknowledgements

Quotations from the Psalms are from the *Book of Common Prayer*. Other biblical quotations are from *The Bible, Revised Standard Version*.

Contents

Preface

There could hardly be two more contrasting descriptions of prayer than George Herbert's 'Prayer, the Church's banquet . . . the land of spices', and R.S. Thomas' 'prayers like gravel flung at the sky's window.' One is pure enjoyment, with a touch of wonder and excitement. The other is an act of desperation and a very chancy thing. For many of us, I suppose, much of our experience and practice of prayer lies between these two extremes – a matter of routine, but without it something significant would be missing from our lives. Sometimes we may find it a hard slog, sometimes we have great rewards, but for much, perhaps for most, of the time, our prayers are an earnest and well-meaning following of repetition and habit. Repetition and habit should not be underrated. They can provide a discipline that is both necessary and beneficial and without them we would lose something of the framework which sustains the duty of prayer. But prayer is a privilege as well as a duty and, if duty alone drives us, our prayers can become impoverished, a one-sided monologue, and the enrichment that comes from the experience of privilege, and from the thanksgiving and joy which that brings, may well be lost.

To enrich prayer is to enrich the whole of life, not just that part of it set aside for 'saying our prayers'. Enrichment comes through seeking a greater awareness of the grace of God at work in our lives, by finding a deeper understanding of the God who is in all things. The title of this book has, deliberately, a double meaning. One sense is that of putting prayer at the very heart of life, not confined to particular times or places, but always responding to the God who is with us. Times of withdrawal, of quiet recollection and reflection as we present ourselves before God, are essential, both for healing and refreshment, but always to bring us back renewed and strengthened to confront the mainstream of life. And the second meaning is in the enlivening of prayer, bringing a sense of newness, of adventure even, giving, not so much new things to say in prayer, as new ways of saying, reflecting fresh insights into the working of God's love in our lives.

Bringing prayer four-square into the totality of life and bringing new life into our prayers are challenges to which we respond in our own different ways. It would be quite wrong to suggest that any one approach would be helpful or beneficial to all. There are many different ways of enriching prayer, and, if the publication of books on prayer is anything to go by, many people are in search of enrichment, are looking for better ways to pray. There are many books of prayers, of which the Church's liturgies are the greatest treasure house; and here I must declare my own love for and dependence upon the Book of Common Prayer, without which my prayers would be greatly impoverished. There are many books of meditations and many, many books telling us how to pray. We must choose what we find helpful and always be conscious that an over-concentration upon the 'how' of prayer may lead us away from the 'why.'

We pray because there is deep within us an inexpressible longing for God, and the God who is within us moves us to respond to him. St Augustine's truth, 'our hearts are restless till they rest in thee', expresses the longing that, to a greater or lesser extent, we seek to articulate in our prayers. One danger is that the very earnestness of our attempts at articulation, especially as we present our intercessions and state our requests and our troubled concerns, can stand in the way of finding a deeper awareness of the workings of God's grace, can reduce our readiness to respond to the Christ who comes to us in and through the lives of others. If we would know more of the generosity of God's grace, more of the richness and diversity of this life which God has given us; if we would have a deeper understanding of the world's pain and sorrow, its joys and celebrations; if we would enter at a deeper level into the relationships that sustain us, whether enduring or fleeting; we would do well to look, not so much to the theologian, the philosopher, the scientist, but to the poet. For it is the poet who takes us into the depths and heights of human experience, who gives us new ways of seeing, who can make a chance observation or chance encounter vibrant with meaning. These are insights we need to bring to our prayers, both to enliven and to enrich.

My purpose is limited – to do no more than share some of the insights gained from a love of poetry, the love of an amateur, an inveterate browser, and as one who finds prayer an imperative of life. That imperative is, for me, a journey and an exploration. All too often, on that journey, and especially when faced with difficulty or worry, or by the sheer wear and tear of the daily grind, I have felt like the servant of Elisha, crying out in some desperation: 'Alas, master, what shall I do?' And Elisha prayed: 'O Lord, open his eyes so that he may see.' (2 Kings 6:17) I can only say that, from time to time and dimly, my eyes have been opened by poetry that has spoken directly to me and that has been both a grace and blessing of life.

CHAPTER 1

Why Poetry and Prayer?

Love's essence, like a poem's, shall spring
From not saying everything
(C. Day Lewis)

Some poems may be used as prayers; some poetry tells us about prayer. Why not leave it at that? One reason is that if we go no further we shall lose opportunities for the deepening and enhancement of prayer. Most of us, I suspect, would welcome some enlivenment of prayer, and it would be foolish not to accept what the poet has to offer. In poetry there is exploration of relationships, of meaning and being, of the world as it is and as it might be, of the depths of the human spirit and, yes, of the delights of trivia, also. The poet is one who is aware, who exposes us to his awareness and, in so doing, enables us to extend our own awareness, gives us new ways of seeing. Listening to the poet can help us listen for God, which is, after all, what so much of prayer ought to be about.

Some poems are prayers; others may set the context for prayer. That wonderful collection of ancient Hebrew poetry, the Psalms, has long been a treasure-trove of prayer. Here the human soul is bared before God; praise and blame; wonder and delight; self-loathing and pride; anger, joy, self-pity – all paraded before God. We draw strength and comfort from some of the Psalms as we use them as prayers and feel, moreover, as we use them, that we are drawn into a broad concourse of prayer beaten hard by continued use down the centuries. Psalms 23, 121 and 84 bring their own comfort and reassurance at times of personal and public need. Other Psalms are cries from the depths of human yearning: 'Save me, O God, for the waters are come in, even unto my soul' (Ps. 69), 'My soul truly waiteth still upon God, for of him cometh my salvation' (Ps. 62), 'Out of the deep have I called unto thee, O Lord. Lord, hear my prayer' (Ps. 130), 'I cried unto the Lord with my voice, I poured out my complaints before him and shewed him my troubles' (Ps. 142). The Psalmist is not afraid to be angry before God, and with God; to call down his wrath upon others. 'Deliver me, O Lord, from the evil man. Let hot burning coals fall upon him' (Ps. 140). There are appeals to the God of the nation: 'O God thou hast cast us out and scattered us. O turn thee unto us again' (Ps. 60). 'Let God arise and let his enemies be scattered' (Ps. 68). 'By the waters of Babylon we sat down and wept when we remembered thee, O Sion' (Ps. 137). And there is, in many of the Psalms, a recurrent note of praise and thanksgiving: 'O give thanks unto the Lord; Praise the Lord O my soul' – an almost constant refrain.

If we would see a powerful link between between poetry and prayer, we need look no further than the Psalms. A.E. Housman reflecting upon the power of the Psalms wrote: 'As for the seventh verse of the forty-ninth Psalm in the Book of Common Prayer, "but no man may deliver his brother, nor make agreement with God for him", that is to me poetry so moving that I can hardly keep my voice steady in reading it.'[1] It is, of course, the poetry of Miles Coverdale he is referring to, not that of the original Hebrew.

But it is a far cry from accepting the Psalms as poetry to accepting poetry as having relevance to our own prayer. The Psalms are religious poetry, written in the context of the recognition of the centrality of God in his world. It has to be said that much of religious poetry, the poetry of religious devotion, is, frankly, feeble stuff as poetry, lacking in imagination and inspiration. Dr Johnson was, for the most part, right: 'The ideas of Christian Theology are too simple for eloquence, too sacred for fiction and too majestic for ornament.' Our theme is not religious verse, it is the much broader, more diffuse one of ways in which the poetic experience might helpfully enlarge our perceptions and so make us more open to God. Elizabeth Jennings tells us something of the poetic experience from the standpoint of the poet as creator, as one who shapes and fashions, one who creates the product which will have a life of its own.

> The poise of time. The history of speech.
> Articulation. Subject brought to heel.
> The poem is filled and animated, rich
> With hints and hopes, with how you wish to feel.
>
> It won't be faked or ever forced. You must
> Seek out its landscape even when it's yours.
> The attitude for you is total trust
> Not of your own but of the poem's powers.
>
> It is a gift, a spell, a fabric wrought
> Seamless. It also is a way to pray
> By which I mean it's ceremonious thought
>
> Spoken through you. You must not let it stray.
> It asks for silence sometimes, won't be bought.
> It's given, yet commands you to obey.[2]

'It also is a way to pray.' The way of the poet points to the way of prayer. There is discipline. ('Subject brought to heel.' 'You must not let it stray.') Whether we use our own words in prayer, or those of others, we must be disciplined, for ever trying to keep at bay, or to control, the endless distractions which derail our prayerful thoughts. Sometimes the discipline becomes an end in itself, a laboured yet swift recital of a form of words. Yet we know how unsatisfactory that is: 'It won't be faked or forced.' We know, too, how jaded our prayer can become, because the landscape has become too familiar, the paths of our prayer so well-trodden that we follow out of mere routine. We need to 'seek out its landscapes', to get beyond duty and rediscover delight in our prayers. And we need, also, perhaps the greatest need of all, to get beyond words, to accept that there are times when words are inadequate, times when we need to feel the 'silence sometimes' and to cherish quiet communion.

Elizabeth Jennings in another poem 'For the Times', throws out two challenges we need to heed as we pray.

> I must go back to the start and to the source,
> Risk and relish, trust my language too,
> For there are messages which need strong powers.
> I tell their tale but rhythm rings them true.
>
> This is a risky age, a troubled time.
> Angry language will not help. I seek
> Intensity of music in each rhyme,
> Each rhythm. Don't you hear the world's heart break?
>
> You must, then, listen, meditate before
> You act. Injustices increase each day
> And always they are leading to a war
>
> And it is ours however far away.
> Language must leap to love and carry fear
> And when most grave yet show us how to play.[3]

Just as the poet must strive for the rhythm that rings true, for the intensity of music in each rhyme, so we, in our prayers, must strive for the truth that is beyond our words. Are we ready to accept the challenge of 'hearing the world's heart break', to go beyond the listing of our intercessions before God and enter into a compassionate sharing of the suffering of others? And, having done that, can we rise to the challenge of living always in the hope of God, our prayers 'leaping to the love' which overcomes fear and which, even in the darkness, brings joy?

The poet struggles with words, what T.S. Eliot called 'the intolerable wrestle with words and meanings.'[4] That's the craftsmanship side of it, the making and remaking, the dismantling and reassembling, the false starts, the unsatisfactory endings. But what drives the mind is the inspiration, the imagination, the seeing, the awareness; for the poet is one who sees things with a fresh eye, who finds new patterns, new landscapes, new images, who uses old words in a new way, startling us, stirring us into a new awareness. Shelley, in his 'A

Defence of Poetry' said 'if no new poets should arise to create afresh the associations which have been . . . disorganized, language will be dead to all the noble purposes of human intercourse.' The poet's task in each new generation is to shock us into new ways of seeing. Yes, we must heed Hosea: 'Take words with you and return to the Lord' (14:2). Words are the inevitable baggage of prayer, sometimes stumbling out incoherently, sometimes a dull, dutiful repetition, sometimes sparse and halting; but always inadequate. For we cannot say everything, even if we know what we want to say. Day Lewis, in his poem 'On Not Saying Everything' draws a parallel between the inadequacy of words both in a poem and in our deepest human relationships. It is just impossible to say everything, to express the totality of human feeling, for communication is but one aspect of 'persons in being' to use John Macmurray's phrase.

> Unwritten poems loom as if
> They'd cover the whole of earthly life.
> But each one, growing, learns to trim its
> Impulse and meaning to the limits
> Roughed out by me, then modified
> In its own truth's expanding light.
> A poem, settling to its form,
> Finds there's no jailer, but a norm
> Of conduct, and a fitting sphere
> Which stops it wandering everywhere.
>
> Love's essence, like a poem's, shall spring
> From the not saying everything.[5]

Words are both bridges and barriers, in human relationships and in our relationship with God in prayer. The poet, one most skilled in the use of words, so often leads us into the silence of wonder and awe, of deep joy or into the deep sorrow of loss or pain, an exposure of ourselves, our concerns, our weakness and our yearnings for the love of God. George Herbert's poem 'Teach me, my God and King', still a popular hymn, has the verse:

A man that looks on glass,
On it may stay his eye;
Or if he pleaseth, thro' it pass,
And then the heav'n espy.[6]

In an earlier version of the poem, he included:

Happy are they that dare
Let in the light to all their actions
And show them as they are.[7]

Prayer is a striving for honesty with 'each venture a new beginning, a raid on the inarticulate',[8] a search for the God who is both hidden and revealed:

in everyday life
it is the plain facts and natural happenings
that conceal God and reveal him to us
little by little under the mind's tooling.[9]

But not only under the mind's tooling, although we must do our own striving. God is made known to us also in the yearning of the spirit, in the opening of the heart and mind to the grace of God, in the offering of ourselves in prayer. The way of the poet, which is one of observation, of sensitivity, amongst the joys and wonder of the world, as well as its dark places, can take us to the heart of meaning and being; can lead us, that is, into prayer.

Sources

1. A.E. Housman, *The Name and Nature of Poetry* (Cambridge, 1933) p.37
2. Elizabeth Jennings, 'The Poem in Itself', *Times and Seasons* (Carcanet, 1992), p.84
3. Ibid. p.82
4. T.S. Eliot: 'East Coker', *Four Quartets*, (Faber and Faber, 1944) p.17
5. C. Day Lewis, 'On Not Saying Everything', *The Complete Poems* (Sinclair-Stevenson, 1992), p.600
6. George Herbert, *The English Poems of George Herbert* (J.M. Dent, 1974), p.188

7. Ibid. p.208

8. T.S. Eliot, op. cit. p.22

9. R.S. Thomas, 'Emerging', *Collected Poems, 1945-1990* (Phoenix, 1993), p.355

CHAPTER II

What is Prayer?

Softness and peace, and joy, and bliss, . . .
The land of spices

(George Herbert)

George Herbert's poem, 'Prayer', opens up a vista of almost infinite possibilities – the challenges of prayer, its rewards, its promises. Here is a vision of prayer as something that demands disciplined hard work and yet is also vibrant with expectancy and excitement.

> Prayer, the Church's banquet, Angel's age,
> God's breath in man returning to his birth,
> The soul in paraphrase, heart in pilgrimage,
> The Christian plummet sounding heaven and earth;
> Engine against the Almighty, sinner's tower,
> Reversed thunder, Christ-side-piercing spear,
> The six-day's world transposing in an hour,
> A kind of tune, which all things hear and fear;
> Softness and peace, and joy, and love, and bliss,
> Exalted manna, gladness of the best,
> Heaven in ordinary, man well drest,
> The milky way, the bird of Paradise,
> Church-bells beyond the stars heard, the soul's blood,
> The land of spices; something understood.[1]

The country that is prayer is frequently barren, a dry and unrewarding landscape; sometimes lively and joyous, and always challenging. There are times when our journey into that country gives refreshment and renewal; other times when we experience emptiness and weariness of spirit. George Herbert's description of prayer as a 'land of spices' may seem far removed from the daily discipline of petition and intercession. Herbert would have us experience prayer as an adventure, as something exciting, exotic even, bringing zest and flavour into our lives, transforming bland ordinariness into an experience of wonder and joy. But even Herbert has another very different description of prayer as an 'Engine against the Almighty' – that continual pounding of God with our requests, those cries from the heart and mind that are desperate for his answers. Prayer as a land of delight is set against a sort of warfare in which we are for ever mustering our demands. Prayer is a paradox. It is a duty and a discipline, a chore, and yet is also an offering freely and readily made. It is a struggle with words and yet is at its most rewarding in silence. For there are times when to be inarticulate is to be most honest. It is a lonely business, between me and God, and yet when we pray we join a great company of souls at prayer. It is an intensely personal offering and a public activity of both intercession and thanksgiving. It is a searching and a coming home.

It is the very paradox of prayer which causes so much frustration. And perhaps the greatest paradox lies in the conflict between withdrawal and engagement. We have a need for times of quiet, for setting aside the tasks, the concerns, the routines of busy, time-ruled lives; times when we can reflect, become more aware of the God who is around us and within us. Times of withdrawal are essential; when we offer our deepest concerns to God, when we seek to make ourselves more open to his presence. Yet prayer, as Alan Ecclestone reminds us, is about engagement and passion and if withdrawal does not encourage engagement with passion, it becomes escapism. 'Praying is engagement, the most far-reaching in intention, the most weighty in implication, the most rich in promise.'[2] Bonhoeffer expresses it passionately: 'I should like to speak to God not on the borders of life, but at its centre.'[3]

Books of instruction and guidance on prayer, which are numberless, add to the frustration. I find, as I read some of them, either a sense of growing irritation with prescriptions of disciplines which I know I shall never, ever, be able to maintain, or a mind-sapping inferiority as I read of the heights of achievement of others in prayer and I have to accept that I have hardly reached the first rung on the ladder. All those aids to meditation and contemplation that are offered – why do they seem to work for others and succeed only in making me more self-conscious rather than God-conscious? All their intensity of prayer and yet I cannot concentrate for two minutes even. I can draw a certain amount of comfort from knowing that John Donne could no more banish the devil distraction than I can:

> I throw my selfe down in my chamber, and I call in, and invite God, and his Angels thither, and when they are there, I neglect God and his Angels for the noise of a Flie, for the ratling of a Coach, for the whining of a doore; I talke on, in the same posture of praying; Eyes lifted up; knees bowed downe, as though I prayed to God; and, if God or his Angels should aske me, when I last thought of God in that prayer, I cannot tell: Sometimes I find that I had forgot what I was about, but when I began to forget it, I cannot tell. A memory of yesterday's pleasures, a feare of tomorrow's dangers, a straw under my knees, a noise in mine eare, a light in mine eye, an anything, a nothing, a fancy, a Chimera in my braine, troubles me in prayer.[4]

Little wonder that he could write: 'Churches are best for prayer that have the least light.'[5]

But I have to accept that John Donne, even with all his distractions could scale greater heights than I and find God within him, which is the essence of prayer.

> Hear us, O hear us Lord . . .
> Hear us, for till thou hear us, Lord,
> We know not what to say . . .
> hear thyself now, for thou in us dost pray.[6]

I know that Julian of Norwich is right when she chides me for spending too much time telling God what I want or need, and telling him what is wrong with the world:

Then the way we often pray came into my mind and how, through lack of knowing and understanding of the ways of love, we pester him with our petitions. Then I saw truly that it gives more praise to God and more delight if we pray steadfast in love, trusting his goodness, clinging to him by grace, than if we ask for everything our thoughts can name. All our petitions fall short of God and are too small to be worthy of him, and his goodness encompasses all that we can think or ask. The best prayer is to rest in the goodness of God knowing that that goodness can reach right down to our lowest depths of need.[7]

I draw comfort from knowing that Julian, too, was not always able to achieve that best prayer, which is resting in the goodness of God. For one senses she was writing from hard experience when she said:

Pray inwardly, even though you find no joy in it. For it does good, though you feel nothing, see nothing, yes, even though you think you cannot pray. For when you are dry and empty, sick and weak, [says God] your prayers please me, though there be little enough to please you. All believing prayer is precious to me.[8]

What are we to make of Herbert, with his 'Prayer – the Church's banquet'? As he stands amazed before the immensity of the riches of prayer, the range of his imagery might well put us off as we struggle to keep going with our lack-lustre prayers. But Herbert, too, in the poem is struggling with the complexities, the paradoxes of prayer. 'The soul in paraphrase, the heart in pilgrimage' – this is where most of us start in prayer. Our 'soul in paraphrase' may well be a hesitant stammering as we seek to find the right words in our prayers; we shall try, over and over again, to find different ways of bringing our needs, our thanks, before God; and we shall use, in constant repetition, words of prayers that are part of our spiritual heritage. As we use those words we shall have to accept that words take us only so far. We shall struggle to be clearer in our thoughts, to be more explicit in our requests; whatever we say is an inadequate expression of our

11

yearning before God. Paraphrase, however well constructed, gives but a partial meaning of the totality we desire to express. We are not to be dispirited about that; it is not the finding of the right words that is important in prayer; it is the finding of ourselves before God. For God's spirit is within us as we pray. It is 'God's breath in man returning to his birth', and our prayer becomes fuller, more complete, more rewarding as we allow the Spirit to work in us. Prayer is never a creation of our own. The more we attempt to make it so, the more we shall be constrained within a narrow and unsatisfying experience of repetition of requests, the less we shall journey on the 'heart's pilgrimage'. If the 'soul in paraphrase' describes something of the development of self-knowledge in our prayer, then the 'heart's pilgrimage' brings us to a knowledge of God. We are, all too often, too narrow in our prayers, sticking to the well-worn paths, never risking that larger exploration of the wider country that is prayer. 'Thou hast set my feet in a large room', the Psalmist says.[9] Our prayer should be an exploration of that large room, a pilgrimage of meditation in which we learn more and more of the love of God and of his sharing with us the paths we walk in – the light and the joy, the darkness and the pain.

In prayer, by self-examination and by self-offering, our perspectives and our horizons change; so do our priorities, part of the process of 'sounding heaven and earth' as the 'Christian plummet' of prayer deepens our perceptions, enlivens our being. It is not a matter of escaping the workaday world, but of transposing our experience of that world into another key, into another 'kind of tune', in which the 'melancholy, long, withdrawing roar'[10] of faith under attack is given a note of reassurance and of joy, even if only momentarily. Herbert's poem ends on a note of paradox. 'The land of spices' brings us to a high note, all wonder and expectation, to a mystery that is welcoming, exciting and full of expectancy. Yet the outcome is only 'something understood'. One might perhaps have hoped for something more, a greater, more complete revelation. But to possess that 'something understood' is to know and to experience the reality of the love of God that is at the heart of prayer and to know the deep reassurance of God with us. Questions remain, many of them, and we must continue to walk through dark places, but the 'something understood' granted in prayer is confirmation of relationship, the affirmation of the words of Jesus, 'Lo, I am with you always', that is made in our lives.

We find a bleaker, chilling view of prayer in R.S. Thomas's 'Folk Tale', the very title expressing the antithesis of the land of spices.

> Prayers like gravel
> Flung at the sky's
> window, hoping to attract
> the loved one's
> attention. But without
> visible plaits to let
> down for the believer
> to climb up,
> to what purpose open
> that far casement?
> I would
> have refrained long since
> but that peering once
> through my locked fingers
> I thought I detected
> the movement of a curtain.[11]

Here is the hard slog of prayer, the great gulf one experiences, a gulf one tries vainly to bridge with cries from the heart. This is the God of whom Isaiah said, 'Truly thou art a God that hidest thyself'.[12] Are we spurred on by thoughts of a momentary twitch of the curtain; is that the full extent of the revelation of 'something understood'? Thomas's world is bleak; his world of the spirit is as hard sometimes as his forbidding Welsh landscape. He is the modern Psalmist calling out in extremity of need, in despair, demanding of God answers to the world's needs and not getting them.

The waves run up the shore
and fall back. I run
up the approaches of God
and fall back. The breakers return
reaching a little further,
gnawing away at the mainland.
They have done this thousands
of years, exposing little by little
the rock under the soil's face.
I must imitate them only
in my return to the assault,
not in their violence. Dashing
my prayers at him will achieve
little other than the exposure
of the rock under the surface.
My returns must be made
on my knees. Let despair be known
as my ebb-tide; but let prayer
have its springs, too, brimming,
disarming him; discovering somewhere
among his fissures deposits of mercy
where trust may take root and grow.[13]

Prayer does have its springs, and they are more rewarding than the mere twitch of a curtain. The 'deposits of mercy where trust may take root and grow' come from the grace of God in our lives. We need a new way of seeing so that we become aware of his grace, of the evidences of his coming into our lives. Part of our trouble, I suppose, is that so much of our conception of the glory of God is caught up with aspects of the might and majesty of a transcendent God. And yet we are more likely to find him in the little epiphanies and in the sorrows as well as the joys. The glory of God was made manifest in the transfiguration of Jesus, but when he prayed, 'Father, the hour has come; glorify thy Son', it heralded the passion of Christ and through that suffering the glory of God was made known. Always, we must keep before us two very different images: of Christ in glory in his transfiguration and ascension and the Christ who put on the towel and washed the feet of his disciples. Prayer is a call to live with and to experience the paradoxes of glory and to see the Christ who

> plays in ten thousand places,
> Lovely in limbs, and lovely in eyes not his
> To the Father through the features of men's faces.[14]

Always we must be ready to respond and to 'greet him the days when I meet him, and bless when I understand'.[15]

'Prayer,' says Harry Williams, 'begins as the opening of heart and mind to God's love',[16] a definition which sits ill with Thomas's gravel flung skywards and his assaults to expose the hard rock of God. John Donne pleads that the assault may be the other way, that our defences may be broken down by the power of the love of God:

> Batter my heart, three personed God; for you
> As yet but knock, breathe, shine, and seek to mend;
> That I may rise, and stand, o'erthrow me, and bend
> Your force, to break, blow, burn and make me new.
> I, like an usurped town to another due,
> Labour to admit you, but Oh, to no end,
> Reason your viceroy in me, me should defend,
> But is captived, and proves weak or untrue.
> Yet dearly I love you, and would be loved fain,
> But am betrothed unto your enemy;
> Divorce me, untie, or break the knot again,
> Take me to you, imprison me, for I
> Except you enthral me, never shall be free,
> Nor ever chaste, except you ravish me.[17]

Donne, dearly though he loves God, faithfully though he labours in his prayers, is imprisoned by his reason, weakened by his failings and can only cry out in anguish with that stark, shocking image of a desire to be ravished by God.

We are likely to be less articulate than Donne, more circumspect in our expectations and desires – and so we keep at it as best we may. The very discipline of our circumspection can blunt our awareness. Sincere prayer is risk; in opening our heart and mind to God we are likely to be caught unawares, our petitions are turned back upon us, our desire for God becomes a personal challenge in the depth of our being, a desire which must be exercised in waiting and watching.

Prayer is like watching for the
Kingfisher. All you can do is
Be where he is likely to appear, and
Wait.
Often, nothing much happens;
There is space, silence and
Expectancy.
No visible sign, only the
Knowledge that he's been there
And may come again.
Seeing or not seeing cease to matter,
You have been prepared.
But when you've almost stopped
Expecting it, a flash of brightness
Gives encouragement.[18]

'Prayer is like watching for the kingfisher.' Anyone who has ever done that knows how tense one becomes in the watching, how quickly observant of the merest flash of light and colour, how expectant. How much of our prayer is like that? That sort of prayer is a world removed from a resigned 'Thy will be done.' Yes, we must be ready to accept that this, rather than that, is the will of God, and we must hope that, in our prayer, we shall come close to knowing and accepting his will. But it is in the tense expectancy of 'watching for the kingfisher' that we catch the flashes of recognition of the grace of God in our lives, and prayer becomes then, not a set time, a set routine, but an experience at the centre of life and at the heart of our being. We find it difficult to accept that 'praying comes not as a problem to be solved, but as a venture to be lived out.'[19] That venture has its own enormous challenges. Being given the strength to live out that venture, which stands at the centre of life, is the real answer to prayer.

> King Christ, this world is all aleak;
> and life-preservers there are none:
> and waves which only He may walk
> Who dares to call himself a man.[20]

Prayer won't quell the waves, but it will give us courage to face them and it will also enable us to recognize, rather than ignore, the 'flash of brightness' which gives encouragement, as in the 'Bright Field' of R.S. Thomas's poem:

> I have seen the sun break through
> to illuminate a small field
> for a while, and gone my way
> and forgotten it. But that was the pearl
> of great price, the one field that had
> the treasure in it. I realize now
> that I must give all that I have
> to possess it. Life is not hurrying
>
> on to a receding future, nor hankering after
> an imagined past. It is the turning
> aside like Moses to the miracle
> of the lit bush, to a brightness
> that seemed as transitory as your youth
> once, but is the eternity that awaits you.[21]

Prayer is a matter of perception, of perception of God's love for me, of priorities for action, of the needs of others and of my own needs. From changed perceptions and deeper understandings flow commitment and action – prayer at work. The sudden illumination that is perception can bring joy and challenge, shame or relief. It does not come to order, but is the breaking through into our consciousness of something hidden or but dimly perceived. Prayer is the turning aside so that we can be open to catch the sudden illumination. To that we must give time. It is precisely the demand for time for prayer which can be so worrying, so off-putting. To read of those great souls who speak of always starting the day with an hour of prayer may give cause for admiration of their single-mindedness, but it is not likely to help us as we struggle with our five or ten minutes as we work against the clock. The two problems are those of finding time and knowing how to use it. Finding time is a matter of priorities. We can go a long way towards satisfying our conscience and, to some extent, our personal needs, by giving over short times to prayer at the beginning and end of each day and by using short times during the day for 'arrow prayers', inner recollection, or whatever. The question to be posed, and answered, is whether we make a deliberate, conscious allocation of priority to time for prayer, the acceptance not of a formality, but of a duty which, if put aside or skipped, leaves the day incomplete, unbalanced, unfulfilled. Of course, we can pray anywhere, at any time and precious indeed are those moments when, at the busiest of times, we acknowledge God's presence with us, when we ask for his guidance, seek his strength. But nothing can or should take the place of that time, short or long, when our thoughts are centred wholly (or as near as we can get to that) upon the one in whom we live and move and have our being.

Knowing how to use the time of prayer is a matter for each one of us individually to resolve. We must pray as we can, not as we can't. There are times when we need no guiding, no instruction; when we perhaps come before God in great anguish of spirit or, perhaps, with an overwhelming sense of joy and thankfulness. At other times, perhaps on most occasions, we need some structure to our prayers. The prescriptions of others may not always help us directly and indeed, can be positively unhelpful, leading to feelings of guilt. 'What did I leave out this morning?' 'Where did I fall down?' 'Was it in my Adoration, or Confession, or Thanksgiving or Supplication? 'Am I progressing from Meditation to Contemplation?' We can certainly profit from the prayer experience of others, but prayer is God in me, in which I come before him, offer myself; an encounter in which I find true freedom. It is the encounter which is all important and it is vital, as part of that encounter, that we should strive to achieve some time of quiet stillness with God, in which we are open to his presence. It is that 'resting in the goodness of God' which makes a time of prayer such a strength to the rest of our living. So we become more perceptive of the grace of God at work in our lives. So we can catch the 'brightness that is the eternity that awaits us'. So our engagement with the world is not a 'hurrying after a receding future, nor a hankering after an imagined past', but becomes the challenge of action to which we are called by love.

Out of the stillness before God comes honesty, with ourselves and with God. For searching continues in the stillness:

> Often I try
> To analyse the quality
> Of its silences. Is this where God hides
> From my searching? I have stopped to listen,
> After the few people have gone,
> To the air recomposing itself
> For vigil. It has waited like this
> Since the stones grouped themselves about it.
> These are the hard ribs
> Of a body that our prayers have failed
> To animate. Shadows advance
> From their corners to take possession
> Of places the light held
> For an hour. The bats resume
> Their business. The uneasiness of the pews
> Ceases. There is no other sound
> In the darkness but the sound of a man
> Breathing, testing his faith
> On emptiness, nailing his questions
> One by one to an untenanted cross.[22]

Prayer is testing our faith, having the courage and the honesty to nail our questions to the cross. R.S. Thomas's honesty can upset us; he sees a bleak world in which God is, all too often, hidden and inaccessible. True, there are moments of revelation, as in the bright field, but they are rare. And yet, in other poems Thomas suggests that it is our lack of perception which is at fault, our slowness to recognize the God who is with us.

> He is such a fast
> God, always before us and
> leaving as we arrive.[23]

And:
> his are the echoes
> We follow, the footprints he has just
> Left.[24]

The 'God of surprises' as Gerard Hughes calls him, is the God who challenges in our lives, the one to whom we pray for help in perceiving those challenges and responding to them.

In nailing questions to an empty cross, we are acknowledging the pain and tragedy of the world and also that Christ, in his passion, shared fully in the pain. But this is not an act of resignation, much less one of capitulation in the face of evil and suffering. The empty cross in Church is a symbol of the evil and pain in the world, but a symbol also of the victory of Christ over that evil.

The trouble with so much unrewarding prayer derives from our narrowing down, our close focusing of thought and feeling into particular channels of intercession and petition. Prayer would not be prayer if we did not ask things of God, if we did not bring before him our deepest needs and the needs of others. But prayer is an opening up also, an opening out of ourselves to God's love, the enlargement of our spirit as we become more and more aware that God is with us, as we become more aware of something of God's glory in the world and more aware also of the truth and reality of the resurrected Christ. At the heart of the Trinity is the human Christ, so that we, in all our humanity, may never be separated from the love of God. Always in our prayer we should be seeking the experience of the Easter Christ, making our plea:

> Let him easter in us, be a dayspring to the dimness of us,
> be a crimson-cresseted east.[25]

It is for something of that light within us, that spirit that both enlightens and enlivens, for which we pray; the Easter Christ who comes to us in the banal ordinariness of the everyday. It is in the 'now' of life that we find the resurrection. Simone Weil has said: 'the effective part of our will is not effort, which is directed towards the future. It is consent; it is the "yes" of marriage. A "yes" pronounced within the present moment and for the present moment, for it is consent to the union of Christ with the eternal part of my soul'.[26]

Edwin Muir in his poem 'Annunciation' earths the encounter between Mary and the angel, quite literally. It could have been any meeting, any day, anywhere. What made it different was the transparent openness of Mary to God, the perfection of her faith and humility.

> The angel and the girl are met.
> Earth was the only meeting place.
> For the embodied never yet
> Travelled beyond the shore of space.
> The eternal spirits in freedom go.
>
> See, they have come together, see,
> While the destroying minutes flow,
> Each reflects the other's face
> Till heaven in hers and earth in his
> Shine steady there. He's come to her
> From beyond the farthest star,
> Feathered through time. Immediacy
> Of strangest strangers is the bliss
> That from their limbs all movement takes.
> Yet the increasing rapture brings
> So great a wonder that it makes
> Each feather tremble on his wings.

Outside the window footsteps fall
Into the ordinary day
And with the sun along the wall
Pursue their unreturning way.
Sound's perpetual roundabout
Rolls its numbered octaves out
And hoarsely grinds its battered tune.

But through the endless afternoon
These neither speak nor movement make,
But stare into their deepening trance
As if their gaze would never break.[27]

In prayer there is, for each of us a promise of an annunciation, however dimly we may be aware of it, however unready or unwilling we may be to respond to it. But whilst we need the stillness, the reflection, we cannot, any more than Mary could, stay indefinitely in tranquil wonder and recollection, isolated from the ever-present world, staring into a 'deepening trance as if their gaze would never break'. The world calls; 'footsteps fall into the ordinary day', and not only does sound 'hoarsely grind its battered tune', but events will not wait; we cannot for long turn aside from involvement. Mary's response was the Magnificat, a reminder, if ever one was needed, of all that needs doing in a world of injustice, inequity and pain. One of St Teresa's prayers is a blunt call to action: 'Christ has no body on earth but ours, no hands but ours, no feet but ours. Ours are the eyes through which must look out Christ's compassion on the world. Ours are the feet with which He is to go about doing good. Ours are the hands with which He is to bless men now'. Perhaps we need to say that prayer at the end of all our intercessions.

Yet, it has not all been left to us to do, with an absentee God expecting us to sort it all out. The Holy Spirit both calls and empowers; we are his instrument for fulfilling the will of God. St Clement of Alexandria, writing in the second century A.D., gives us a striking image of what it means to be the image of God and his instrument:

The Word of God,
born of David's line yet older than David,
disdaining lyre and harp, mindless instruments,
tuned the cosmos to himself by the Holy Spirit,
especially that tiny cosmos, man, mind and body.
On this many-voiced instrument he plays to God,
and sings to his instrument man.
'You are a harp for me, a flute and a shrine':
a harp by your fine-strung harmony,
a flute by your breath,
a shrine by your reason.
Let the harp resound to his touch,
the flute breathe his living Breath
and the shrine be the home for the Lord . . .
A beautiful, breathing instrument has God fashioned man,
after his own image,
for divine Wisdom, the heavenly Logos, is himself God's instrument,
harmonious, apt for all melodies,
delicate and holy . . .
What is it, his new song?
To shed light on blind eyes,
to open deaf ears,
to take the limping and the strays by hand and lead them aright,
to stem corruption and conquer death,
to reconcile disobedient sons to their Father.
For God's instrument is in love with man.[28]

Mary was the perfect instrument of God, responding faithfully in tune, in perfect harmony. Perhaps if we can only manage the occasional note, expressed as action for God's compassion and justice, our prayer will have been fulfilled.

'Home,' wrote T.S. Eliot, 'is where one starts from'.[29] Likewise, prayer is where one starts from; as we pray so we are. But prayer is also a coming home, a finding of ourselves before God.

> Home is the place where, when you have to go there,
> They have to take you in.
>   I should have called it
> Something you somehow haven't to deserve.[30]

George Herbert's poem, 'Love', is about the welcome of the Holy Communion, but applies equally to the welcome which awaits us in prayer. 'Our Lord', says Julian of Norwich, 'is greatly cheered by our prayer. He looks for it, and wants it'.[31] He wants to speak in us, to shape our petitions, to enlarge our perceptions, to make us more receptive to his grace. He wants us to feel at home with him in prayer.

> Love bade me welcome: yet my soul drew back,
>> Guilty of dust and sin.
> But quick-eyed Love, observing me grow slack
>> From my first entrance in,
> Drew nearer to me, sweetly questioning,
>> If I lacked any thing.
>
> A guest, I answered, worthy to be here:
>> Love said, You shall be he.
> I the unkind, the ungrateful? Ah my dear,
>> I cannot look on thee.
> Love took my hand, and smiling did reply,
>> Who made the eyes but I?
>
> Truth Lord, but I have marred them: let my shame
>> Go where it doth deserve.
> And know you not, says Love, who bore the blame?
>> My dear, then I will serve.
> You must sit down, says Love, and taste my meat:
>> So I did sit and eat.[32]

The comforting vision of a warmth of welcome, of an easy sustaining relationship with God is all of a piece with Herbert's other image of prayer as the Church's banquet. Even R.S. Thomas, the bleakest of poets, has his moments of glory, moving, as it were, into Herbert's country, at home with the God who takes us in and fills us:

> As I had always known
> he would come, unannounced,
> remarkable merely for the absence
> of clamour...

> I looked
> at him, not with the eye
> only, but with the whole
> of my being, overflowing with
> him as a chalice would
> with the sea.[33]

But Thomas, as ever, will not let us rest in quiet withdrawal. His chalice reminds of passion and sacrifice and suffering. And he goes on in the same poem to talk of 'unhaloed presences', of 'gamblers at the foot of the unnoticed cross'. For prayer does not take us out of the world, it strengthens us for the world, not that we may accept the world as it is, but that we shall come closer to an understanding of the power of love in the world.

Sources

1. George Herbert, 'Prayer', *The English Poems of George Herbert*, p.70
2. Alan Ecclestone: *Yes to God*, (Darton, Longman and Todd, 1975), p.9
3. Dietrich Bonhoeffer, *Letters and Papers from Prison*, (Collins, Fontana, 1959), p.93
4. Stevie Davies, *John Donne*, (Northcote House, 1994), p.59
5. John Donne, 'A Hymn to Christ at the Author's last going into Germany', *The Works of John Donne*, (Wordsworth Poetry Library, 1994) p.272
6. 'The Litanie' XXIII, ibid., p.267
7. Julian of Norwich, *Enfolded in Love* (Darton, Longman and Todd, 1980) p.5
8. Ibid., p.20
9. Psalm 31:9
10. Matthew Arnold, 'Dover Beach', *Poems*, (J.M. Dent, 1965), p.226
11. R.S. Thomas, 'Folk Tale', *Collected Poems*, p. 517
12. Isaiah, 45:15
13. R.S. Thomas, 'Tidal', *Mass for Hard Times*, (Bloodaxe, 1992), p.43

14. G.M. Hopkins, 'As kingfishers catch fire', *The Poems of Gerard Manley Hopkins*, (Oxford University Press, 1948), p.90
15. 'The Wreck of the Deutschland', ibid., p.53
16. H.A. Williams, *Becoming what I am*, (Darton, Longman and Todd, 1977), ii
17. John Donne, 'Holy Sonnets XIV', *Poems and Devotions*, (Harper Collins, Fount, 1995), p.51
18. Anne Lewin, 'Disclosure', *The Lion Christian Poetry Collection*, (1995), p.16
19. Alan Ecclestone, op. cit., p.8
20. e.e. cummings, *Selected Poems 1923-1958*, (Faber and Faber, 1968) p.32
21. R.S. Thomas, 'The Bright Field', *Collected Poems*, p.302
22. R.S. Thomas, 'In Church', ibid., p.180
23. R.S. Thomas, 'Pilgrimage', ibid., p.364
24. R.S. Thomas, 'Via Negativa', ibid., p.220
25. G.M. Hopkins, 'The Wreck of the Deutschland', op. cit., p.63
26. Simone Weil, 'Concerning the Our Father'; *Waiting on God*, (Collins Fontana, 1959), p.171
27. Edwin Muir, 'The Annunciation', *Collected Poems*, (Faber and Faber, 1984), p.223
28. Clement of Alexandria, in Maria Boulding, *Marked for Life*, (SPCK, 1995) p.69
29. T.S. Eliot, 'East Coker', *The Four Quartets*, p.22
30. Robert Frost, 'Death of the Hired Man', *Selected Poems*, (Penguin, 1955), p.38
31. Julian of Norwich, *Revelations of Divine Love*, (Penguin, 1966) p.124
32. George Herbert: 'Love III', *Poems*, p.192
33. R.S. Thomas, 'Suddenly', *Collected Poems*, p.283

CHAPTER III

Coming to God

Our prayer seems lost in desert ways,
Our hymn in the vast silence dies
(G.M. Hopkins)

We come to God in prayer in many different ways. We come in our need, bringing our anxieties, our pain and our hurt. We come in thanksgiving and joy, in doubt and fear, in shame and guilt. We come with a longing to find and to know God and we come in weariness and emptiness at not finding him. Sometimes we are moved to reverence and awe by some vision of nature or by man-made beauty, or the stillness of a holy place. Always we come to him as we are and where we are. We shall offer our prayers in our own words, sometimes wrung from the heart, sometimes as a duty to be quickly done; we shall use the words of others to carry our thoughts. More often than not, our prayers are rough, unfinished things, notable only for the depth of feeling that lies behind the words. Elizabeth Jennings compares her prayer to van Gogh's 'Crooked Church', a crazy, seemingly meaningless construction.

> Maybe a mad fit made you set it there
> Askew, bent to the wind, the blue-print gone
> Awry, or did it? Isn't every prayer
> We say oblique, unsure, seldom a simple one,
> Shaken as your stone tightening the air?
>
> Decorum smiles a little. Columns, domes
> Are sights, are aspirations. We can't dwell
> For long among such loftiness. Our homes
> Of prayer are shaky and, yes, parts of Hell
> Fragment the depths from which the great cry comes.[1]

When words are inadequate we shall come in silence and find that it is there that we come closest to God. One of Dom John Chapman's spiritual letters has messages for all of us:

> ... the only way to pray is to pray; and the way to pray well is to pray much. If one has no time for this, then one must at least pray regularly. But the less one prays, the worse it goes. And if circumstances do not permit even regularity, then one must put up with the fact that when one does try to pray, one can't pray – and our prayer will probably consist of telling this to God ... As to religious matters being 'confused and overwhelming', I dare say they may remain so – in a sense – but if you get the right simple relation to God by prayer, you have got into the centre of the wheel, where the revolving does not matter. We can't get rid of the worries of this world, or of the questionings of the intellect; but we can laugh at and despise them so far as they are worries.[2]

I don't know about 'laughing at and despising' my worries. Rather, do I want to feel that there is some way through them and that I shall be given strength to cope. If only we could feel and know that we were, truly, coming to God! Echoing the Psalmist with his 'Why standest thou so far off, O Lord?',[3] Gerard Manley Hopkins looks for response:

> God, though to Thee our psalm we raise
> No answering voice comes from the skies;
> To Thee the trembling sinner prays
> But no forgiving voice replies;
> Our prayer seems lost in desert ways,
> Our hymn in the vast silence dies.
>
> And Thou art silent, whilst Thy world
> Contends about its many creeds
> And hosts confront with flags unfurled
> And zeal is flushed and pity bleeds
> And truth is heard, with tears impearled,
> A moaning voice among the reeds.
>
> Speak! whisper to my watching heart
> One word – as when a mother speaks

Soft, when she sees her infant start,
Till dimpled joy steals o'er its cheeks.
Then, to behold Thee as Thou art,
I'll wait till morn eternal breaks.[4]

In another of his poems it is with a cry of terror almost that he seeks God, overwhelmed by his feeling of separation:

Comforter, where is your comforting?
Mary, mother of us, where is your relief? . . .
O the mind, mind has mountains; cliffs of fall
Frightful, sheer, no-man-fathomed. Hold them cheap
May who ne'er hung there.[5]

Prayer is an attempt to overcome the separation from God which we all experience. There are times when, to pray 'Our Father who art in heaven', underlines the separation, placing God 'out there'. And, instead of praying in confidence and trust to the God who watches over us in his wisdom and power, who is very near to us, we feel, rather, the gulf between ourselves and God as we vainly try to bridge it. It is in these times especially that we must hold on in faith to the words of Psalm 139: 'O Lord thou hast searched me out and known me . . . Thou art about my path . . . If I take the wings of the morning and remain in the uttermost parts of the sea, even there also shall thy hand lead me; and thy right hand shall hold me.' Our Lord put it even more graphically: 'Even the hairs of your head are all numbered' (Luke 12:7.) God is near to us, within us and always seeking us. Our prayer must be an offering, not just of our petitions, but of ourselves, to the God who truly comes to us.

O Lord, seek us, O Lord, find us
In thy patient care;
By thy love before, behind us,
Round us everywhere:
Lest the god of this world blind us,
Lest he speak us fair,
Lest he forge a chain to bind us,

> Lest he bait a snare.
> Turn not from us, call to mind us,
>   Find, embrace us, bear;
> Be thy love before, behind us,
>   Round us, everywhere.[6]

The process of trying to find that love, 'before, behind us, round us, everywhere' is, for most of us a mixture of hard slog, the perfunctory, and the sudden moments of reassurance and illumination. And, all too often, it is, consciously, our own driving effort that sustains our prayer. Coming to God, for too much of the time, is a matter of the will, which is not always very strong. But, even when not very strong, my own will, with its insistence upon my priorities, stands in the way of my exposure to God. We are too determined to follow our own way in prayer.

> Prayer [should] become less an effort to love God, and more a matter of letting him love you. Relax, because he loves you. To be preoccupied with your own unworthiness is not only pointless but obstructive. It is very humbling to be loved by someone who knows everything and still loves you, as Peter discovered on the lakeside after the resurrection. The love that knows us is creative, and so to let ourselves be known and loved in prayer is to allow ourselves to be changed.[7]

Julian of Norwich in her *Revelations* writes much of prayer, whilst avoiding any prescriptions as to method. Wisely, she focuses upon God, not upon how we organize our prayers, our posture, our time. In Julian's writings we perceive three processes, or aspects, of prayer – longing, asking, contemplating – which arise quite naturally in our approach to God. Julian is not telling us that there is a required sequence of prayer whereby we progress from longing for God to contemplation of him. She does not set up hurdles in prayer, nor stages proceeding, as it were, from elementary to advanced. She helps us to understand the richness of prayer and urges us to participate in that richness by being prepared to venture in faith into a relationship in which we rest in

God, for, indeed, it is he who prays in us. Longing for God comes from God. 'I am he who makes you to love. I am he who makes you to long. I am the endless fulfilling of all true desires.'[8] Yet all too often, my longing is for things I want from God. I am more comfortable at that level. The 'dart of longing love',[9] the desire for God himself, expressed in St Augustine's prayer, that 'our hearts are restless till they rest in thee', can unsettle, disturb us.

> Notwithstanding that our Lord God lives in us, and is here with us; notwithstanding that he clasps and enfolds us in his tender love, never to leave us; notwithstanding that he is nearer to us than tongue and heart can think and tell, the fact remains that that we shall never cease from sighs, complaints, or tears – or longing – till we see clearly his blessed face. In that precious, blessed sight, no grief can live, no blessing fail.[10]

The pain of longing is something we experience keenly in our human situations; so also it must be in our coming to God. The more we highlight our wants in our prayers, the greater the danger of suppressing longing for God. It is the longing for God, the spirit of God that is deep within us, which will break through the most structured prayer life. 'For we come to God by love, not by navigation, and not even the best charts can of themselves take us to the harbour where we would be.'[11]

Longing, yearning, for God should be a joyous thing, not a melancholy regret. Robert Graves catches something of the joy of longing in a little verse of his:

> Love without hope, as when the young bird-catcher
> Swept off his tall hat to the Squire's own daughter,
> So let the imprisoned larks escape and fly
> Singing about her head, as she rode by.[12]

Our longing for God should have within it something of the joy and wonder of release as our deep desires are caught up with a vision of love. Our relationship with God is not, however, one of love without hope, for our longing comes from God and is fulfilled in him.

Sometimes it is the beauty, the wonder, of the natural world which can inspire us to prayer, infusing us with longing for God, spurring us to worship the God who is both beyond and within us.

> The world is charged with the grandeur of God.
>   It will flame out, like shining from shook foil;
>   It gathers to a greatness, like the ooze of oil
> Crushed.[13]

The grandeur can break through at any time, in the most unlikely places:

> And all is seared with trade; bleared, smeared with toil;
> And wears man's smudge and shares man's smell: the soil
> Is bare now, nor can foot feel, being shod.

> And, for all this, nature is never spent;
> There lives the dearest freshness deep down things . . . [14]

Finding that 'dearest freshness' is a part of the grace of God in our lives, and when we find it, we are moved to praise:

> Glory be to God for dappled things –
>   For skies of couple-colour as a brinded cow;
>   For rose-moles all in stipple upon trout that swim;
>   Fresh-firecoal chestnut-falls; finches' wings;
>   Landscape plotted and pieced – fold, fallow, and plough;
> And all trades, their gear and tackle and trim . . .

>   He fathers-forth whose beauty is past change:
>   Praise him.[15]

We find often enough that the quiet communion which we seek with God may be experienced more deeply among the beauties of nature than in our daily prayers. We should cherish those times and draw upon them in our less exalted moments.

> There is much comfort in high hills
> and a great easing of the heart.
> We look upon them and our nature fills

with loftier images from their life apart.
They set our feet on curves of freedom, bent
to snap the circles of our discontent.

Mountains are moods; of larger rhythms and line,
moving between the eternal mode and mine.
Moments of thought, of which I too am part,
I lose in them my instant of brief ills.
There is a great easing of the heart,
And cumulance of comfort on high hills.[16]

Prayer as duty and discipline will seem all too unlikely at times
to set our feet on 'curves of freedom', nor may it give us 'great
easing of the heart.' Yet it is through the regular duty and
discipline, in which we bring ourselves before God, that we are
made more aware of the coming of God to us in so many different
ways, whether it is in a vision of transcendence in the mountains
and hills, or in the less inspiring things around us. 'He addresses
me from a myriad directions', says R.S. Thomas:

Suddenly after long silence
he has become voluble.
He addresses me from a myriad
directions with the fluency
of water, the articulateness
of green leaves: and in the genes,
too, the components
of my existence. The rock,
so long speechless, is the library
of his poetry. He sings to me
in the chain-saw, writes
with the surgeon's hand
on the skin's parchment messages
of healing. The weather
is his mind's turbine
driving the earth's bulk round
and around on its remedial
journey. I have no need

> to despair; as at
> some second Pentecost
> of a Gentile, I listen to the things
> round me: weeds, stones, instruments,
> the machine itself, all
> speaking to me in the vernacular
> of the purposes of One who is.[17]

We do not have to have the isolated majesty of hills or the high moments of worship, or the cloister of private prayer to receive and acknowledge God. He speaks to us 'in the vernacular of the purposes of One who is'. We can cultivate prayer as openness to God anywhere, at any time. Not by deliberately withdrawing into ourselves – although there will be times when we find that both helpful and necessary – but by being ready to receive the world in thankfulness. The vernacular will then speak to us of joy and of sorrow, of little, seemingly inconsequential things and of matters that are too great to bear. When we are open to the vernacular of God, prayer becomes as natural as breathing; the expected and constant accompaniment of the day. Thomas Traherne is truly the apostle of wonder, the man for whom the everyday is the home of the glory of God.

> Some things are little on the outside and rough and common. But I remember the time, when the dust of the streets was as precious as gold to my infant eyes, and now it is more precious than the eye of reason ... I give thee thanks for the beauty of colours, for the harmony of sounds, for the pleasantness of odours, for the sweetness of food, for the warmth and softness of our raiment, and for all my five senses and all the pores of my body, so curiously made, and for the preservation as well as the use of all my limbs and senses.[18]

But for most people it is too much to ask that the 'daily round, the common task' shall always be infused with prayer. It is enough to ask that there shall be moments of awareness, brief snatches of recollection of the presence of God, a silent invocation, 'To God, be thanks', or a back-of-the-mind appeal,

'Help me, God'. Yet however much we may feel separated from the God who is around us and within us – separated by the pressures and concerns of our busyness – we shall find, still, that prayer is invoked by the significance of place. There are places which, for us, bring us closer to God, by bringing us closer to our true selves. They need not be, and commonly are not, places of particular veneration; they will be, for us, in Kathleen Raine's phrase, 'where it is always now'.

> I have come back to ancient shores where it is always now.
> The beautiful troubled waters breaking over the skerry
> On the wind in spindrift blown like lifting hair,
> Clouds gathering over the summits of Rhum in the clear blue
> Are as they were
> When long ago I went my way in sorrow.
> Time, measure of absence, is not here –
> In the wide present of the sky
> Fleet the broadcast light is already returning, while we,
> Who tell the hours and days by the beat of a heart
> Can only depart
> After a vanishing radiance dragging mortal feet.
> But joy outspeeds light's wheel, the moments in their flight
> Stays, here where in patterned strands the weed holds fast to the shore,
> Falls and lifts from ebb to flow
> Of the unceasing tide that makes all things new,
> And the curlew with immortal voices cry.[19]

Eliot's phrase, 'here, where prayer has been valid'[20], has passed into the language. It tells of places steeped in holiness, which compel reverence. Yet the church at Little Gidding, of which he wrote, is no architectural jewel; it has neither beauty of adornment, nor exquisite form. It is, as a building, plain and ordinary. Yet Eliot is right; there is a felt association which invites to prayer and worship. We are brought to God by the reverence of place. We don't need soaring pillars, vaulted ceilings, vistas of ancient arches, although they will move us greatly on occasions.

It may well be the quiet of a plain country church, the trick of light in some dusty corner which calls us into an awareness which passes into prayer.

> A little window, obscure,
> A flask of water on the vestry press,
> A ray of sunshine through a fretted door,
> And myself kneeling in live quietness.
>
> Heaven's brightness was then gathered in the glass,
> Marshalled and analysed, as one by one
> In terms of fire I saw the colours pass,
> Each in its proper beauty, while the sun
>
> Made his dear daughter Light sing her own praise,
> (As Wisdom may, who is a mode of light),
> Counting her seven great jewels; then those rays
> Remerged in the whole diamond, total sight.
>
> This globe revolved subservient : that just star
> Whirled in his place; water and glass obeyed
> The laws appointed : with them, yet how far
> From their perfection, I still knelt and prayed.[21]

Philip Larkin, not a believer, could, nevertheless, not escape the compelling ambience of place. Not drawn to prayer, he was pulled towards a recognition of reverence of a sort, was brought to a reflection upon human purpose. We might call it the intrusion of the spiritual into the ordinariness of a cyclist's visit to a country church

> Once I am sure there's nothing going on
> I step inside, letting the door thud shut.
> Another church: matting, seats, and stone,
> And little books; sprawlings of flowers, cut
> For Sunday, brownish now; some brass and stuff
> Up at the holy end; the small neat organ;
> And a tense, musty, unignorable silence,
> Brewed God knows how long. Hatless, I take off
> My cycle clips in awkward reverence.

> A serious house on serious earth it is,
> In whose blent air all our compulsions meet,
> Are recognized, and robed as destinies,
> And that much never can be obsolete,
> Since someone will forever be surprising
> A hunger in himself to be more serious,
> And gravitating with it to this ground,
> Which, he once heard, was proper to grow wise in,
> If only that so many dead lie around.[22]

'Since someone will forever be surprising a hunger in himself to be more serious', describes very well aspects of prayer heightened by the reverence of place – the recognition that there are some things that matter so much that they are beyond our power to resolve or fully to understand; and the desire to dig deeper, to establish a firmer foundation for life. Just as respect and veneration in a church may be superficially based – 'if only that so many dead lie around' – so prayer can remain at the level of presenting our wants to God and not getting beyond that. When a place is experienced as possessing holiness, by which I mean that it invokes reverence and awe, it will take us beyond intercession and petition, towards Julian's contemplating or beholding. A holy place is wherever we are brought to a longing, a yearning, which leads to an experience, whether momentary or half-glimpsed, of the numinous, of someone other in our midst. That experience does not come to order; the request on the church door that we should pray as we enter or leave; the hallowed beauty of the building; the glow of the cross on the altar – these things do not always register. There are times when prayer, if it comes at all, will be perfunctory or when the lighting of a candle becomes a mechanical reaction, something we do because it is the done thing. At other times we shall deliberately turn aside from the pressures of the day to enter a church and pray, helped in that prayer by the quiet, by the vague but compelling assurance that 'here prayer has been valid'. But stones can speak and call us, inspire us with some chance reflection leading into deeper truth, which is itself prayer. Larkin has the eye of the poet, caught by the tenderness of stone effigies, man and wife hand in hand in their centuries' old rigid posture. That gentle touch of hand on hand is what survives for Larkin, not the history of an earl and countess, but the strength, the permanence, of human love. Offering that reflection to God would be prayer enough.

> Side by side, their faces blurred,
> The earl and countess lie in stone,
> Their proper habits vaguely shown
> As jointed armour, stiffened pleat,
> And that faint hint of the absurd –
> The little dogs under their feet.
>
> Such plainness of the pre-baroque
> Hardly involves the eye, until
> It meets his left-hand gauntlet, still
> Clasped empty in the other; and
> One sees, with a sharp tender shock,
> His hand withdrawn, holding her hand . . .
>
> Rigidly they
> Persisted, linked, through lengths and breadths
> Of time. Snow fell, undated. Light
> Each summer thronged the glass. A bright
> Litter of birdcalls strewed the same
> Bone-riddled ground. And up the paths
> The endless altered people came . . .
>
> Time has transfigured them into
> Untruth. The stone fidelity
> They hardly meant has come to be
> Their final blazon, and to prove
> Our almost-instinct almost true:
> What will survive of us is love.[23]

But mostly we come to God, not through a sense of place, nor through natural beauty, but through our need, whether as a cry of anguish from a deeply troubled heart or as the bothersome bundle of minor worries and anxieties that make up the normal day. We shall come to God deeply questioning – Why, O Lord?, or despairing in our weakness we shall only be able to pray – Please, Lord! The mysterious road of need and suffering that we walk in faith is, for most of us, never free of doubt and fear. Prayers of intercession are both the easiest and the most difficult to pray. Easy, because our wants spring to the fore, almost unbidden, when we pray. We want to unburden ourselves before God; we want to bring before him those people, those situations, for whom and for which we see desperate needs to be met, needs which lie heavy upon our hearts. We may have difficulty in putting our deepest fears into words, but that will not stop us praying. But intercessory prayer is also very difficult, since we shall be uncertain about its outcome and, all too often perhaps, we shall feel that our prayers go unanswered. And what are we trying to do, anyway? Tell God something that he is not already aware of? Trying to change his mind? Impress upon God what we want? I have not come across a truly satisfying theology of intercessory prayer and I have to accept that here is a mystery to be lived with.

What I accept is that it is in prayer that I expose the essentials of me as a person, with nothing hidden and, however inadequately I express myself in prayer, it is the essential me which ultimately comes through. Any expression of the essential me is impossible without reference to all those relationships which make up and complete my personhood. It would be quite unthinkable that I could be wanting to come to God without sharing with him my concerns for other persons. What I am doing in prayer is bringing them before him so that they are as much in his presence at that time as I am. I can only say that, when I have had times of great need, and my own prayers at such times have felt barren, pointless almost, I have been conscious of being strongly upheld by the prayers of others.

'We pray because there is pain and love in life, because we both suffer and rejoice, because we try to find meaning in it, because we want to share this with another'.[24] Having brought a person before God in our prayers we cannot leave them there. Our love for them keeps its costly vigil, and our service, in love, becomes an exercise in self-giving. We pray for them because we feel that God's love will surely do no less. 'Each time you take a human soul with you into your prayer', writes Evelyn Underhill, 'you accept from God a piece of spiritual work with all its implications and all its cost – a cost which may mean for you spiritual exhaustion and darkness . . . In offering yourselves on such levels of prayer for the sake of others, you are offering to take your part in the mysterious activities of the spiritual world; to share the saving work of Christ. Real intercession is not merely a petition but a piece of work, involving perfect, costly self-surrender to God for the work he wants done on other souls.'[25]

When Jesus walked into the wilderness
he carried a man on his back,
at least it had the form of a man,
a fisherman perhaps with a wet nose,
a baker perhaps with flour in his eyes.
The man was dead it seems
and yet he was unkillable.
Jesus carried many men
yet there was only one man –
if indeed it was a man . . .

For forty days, for forty nights
Jesus put one foot in front of the other
and the man he carried,
if it was a man,
became heavier and heavier.
He was carrying all the trees of the world
which are one tree.
He was carrying forty moons
which are one moon.

He was carrying all the boots
of all the men in the world
which are one boot.
He was carrying our blood.
One blood.

To pray, Jesus knew,
is to be a man carrying a man.[26]

To carry others in our prayers is a costly effort; in our own inadequate way we are doing the work of Christ, which is nothing if not dearly bought. And what we seek from that effort is the gift of newness of life for those for whom we pray; the gift of hope in darkness, of ease in pain, of the recovery of greenness. George Herbert beautifully and powerfully catches the freshness of the grace of God which breaks through the darkness of life.

> How fresh, O Lord, how sweet and clean
> Are thy returns! ev'n as the flowers in spring;
>   To which, besides their own demean,
> The late-past frosts tributes of pleasure bring.
>   Grief melts away
>   Like snow in May,
> As if there were no such cold thing.
>
> Who would have thought my shrivel'd heart
> Could have recover'd greenness? It was gone
>   Quite underground; as flowers depart
> To see their mother-root, when they have blown;
>   Where they together
>   All the hard weather,
> Dead to the world, keep house unknown.
>
> These are thy wonders, Lord of power,
> Killing and quickning, bringing down to hell
>   And up to heaven in an hour;
> Making a chiming of a passing bell.
>   We say amisse,
>   This or that is;
> Thy word is all, if we could spell.[27]

'Thy word is all, if we could spell'; the great 'if only' of prayer. It was George Herbert also who described prayer as 'something understood'. It is that understanding we crave in our coming to

God, so that we may be able to make sense of the world, of our place in it and of all the seeming inconsistencies, injustices and pointless tragedies. 'Part of the Spirit's gift is discernment'[28] – discernment, rather than understanding; the perception that love sustains but does not take over, that the power of God, in love, is seen in the vulnerability of Jesus on the Cross; that the recovery of greenness is in the resurrection by way of the Cross.

A step on the road to our own recovery of greenness is a spirit of true contrition, the bringing before God of our own broken-ness. We may be moved to contrition by the 'acknowledgement and bewailing of our manifold sins and wickedness', but also in surprising ways by things of seemingly little consequence:

> Dew on snowdrop
> >weep for me
> Rain in a rose
> >cleanse my heart,
> Bud of crocus
> >candle me to
> Contrition. Far stars
> >shine from your great
> Heights, and burn my faults away.
> Half-moon emerging
> >from a cloud
> Strengthen my spirit.
> >All spring flowers,
> More each day,
> >in this night now
> Give me a scent of our sweet powers.
> A shower of rain
> >wash me clean,
> Let my spirit glow
> >for I have seen
> The terrible depth
> >of dark in me.
> Christ, you alone
> >can cure jealousy.[29]

In contrition, as in intercession, we need to go beyond a recital of concerns. Prayer is coming close to God and we shall come closest to him in silence. 'There should be in the soul,' said Jeremy Taylor, 'halls of space, avenues of leisure, and high porticoes of silence where God walks'. Silence is indeed the great therapy.

> God is the friend of silence . . . We need to find God and he cannot be found in noise and restlessness . . . Silence gives us a new outlook on everything. We need silence to be able to touch souls. The essential thing is not what we say but what God says to us and through us. Jesus is always waiting for us in silence. In that silence he will listen to us, there he will speak to our soul, and there we will hear his voice. Interior silence is very difficult but we must make the effort. In silence we will find new energy and true unity. The energy of God will be ours to do all things well. The unity of our thoughts with his thoughts, the unity of our prayers with his prayers, the unity of our actions with his actions, of our life with his life.[30]

For most of us, I would suppose, the notion of 'what God says to us in silence' is troublesome. Inner voices, in any case, are suspect. Yet, again and again, we are told by writers on prayer and by great Christian souls, most of whom are very down to earth characters, that prayer is about listening.

> The most difficult and decisive part of prayer is acquiring [the] ability to listen. Listening is no passive affair, a space when we happen not to be doing or speaking. Inactivity and superficial silence do not necessarily mean that we are in a position to listen. Listening is a conscious, willed action, requiring alertness and vigilance, by which our whole attention is focused and controlled. Listening in this sense is a difficult thing. And it is decisive because it is the beginning of our entry into a personal and unique relationship with God, in which we hear the call of our own special responsibilities for which God has intended us. Listening is the aspect of silence in which we receive the commission of God . . . Silence is the matrix of eternity.[31]

What we are seeking, in the silence, are not words from God, but an inner awareness of his presence, a presence which illuminates, gives us a clearer perception of, our prayer. Here we begin to move with that discernment which is the gift of the Spirit. Listening brings 'something understood'.

Whether in silence or in words we shall wish, in our prayers, to give thanks for blessings received, for hope renewed, for the opportunity and the relief of sharing things with God. Our thanksgivings also bring discernment, perhaps of the fragment of a pattern in our lives, of an answer to prayer which we perceive belatedly. We become aware of the 'bright necklace' of God's grace at work in our lives.

> I count the moments of my mercies up,
> I make a list of love and find it full.
> I do all this before I fall asleep.
>
> Others examine consciences. I tell
> My beads of gracious moments shining still.
> I count my good hours and they guide me well
>
> Into a sleepless night. It's when I fill
> Pages with what I think I am made for,
> A life of writing poems. Then may they heal
>
> The pain of silence for all those who stare
> At stars as I do but are helpless to
> Make the bright necklace. May I set ajar
>
> The doors of closed minds. Words come and words go
> And poetry is pain as well as passion.
> But in the large flights of imagination
>
> I see for one crammed second, order so
> Explicit that I need no more persuasion.[32]

In all our prayers, in our coming to God, we want, desperately, reassurance and renewal, we long for the 'crammed second' of enlightenment. Yet what we bring to God matters so much, and W.H. Auden points us to a truth we must learn:

> In the deserts of the heart,
> Let the Healing fountain start,
> In the prison of his days
> Teach the free man how to praise.[33]

We must bring our praise and thanksgiving to God. As we learn to do that, we shall find that the 'healing fountain' starts. St Paul's instruction was 'always and for everything, give thanks in the name of our Lord Jesus Christ to God the Father.'[34] It is only by God's good grace that we can accept the enormity of the challenge of those words. It is in and through our prayers that we shall find that our thankfulness and praise are the natural response to finding God's love.

Sources

1. Elizabeth Jennings, 'The Nature of Prayer', *Collected Poems*, (Carcanet, 1986) p.119
2. *The Spiritual Letters of Dom John Chapman*, ed. Roger Hudleston, (Sheed and Ward, 1946), p.52-53
3. Psalm 10:1
4. G.M. Hopkins, 'Nondum', *The Poems of Gerard Manley Hopkins*, p.32
5. Ibid., p.100
6. Christina Rossetti, *Verses*, (SPCK, 1894), p.121
7. Maria Boulding, *Marked for Life*, (SPCK, 1995) p.33
8. Julian of Norwich, *Revelations of Divine Love*, ed. E. Colledge and J. Walsh, (Paulist Press, 1978) p.296
9. *The Cloud of Unknowing*, trans. Clifford Wolters, (Penguin, 1961), Chapter 6
10. Julian of Norwich, *Revelations of Divine Love*, (Penguin, 1966), p.190
11. Robert Llewelyn, *With Pity not with Blame*, (Darton, Longman and Todd, 1982), p.83
12. Robert Graves, *Poems on the Underground*, (Cassell, 1991), p.113
13. G.M. Hopkins, op. cit., p.66
14. Ibid., p.66

15. Ibid., p.69
16. Geoffrey Winthrop Young, 'High Hills' in Alan Ecclestone, *Gather the Fragments* (Cairns Publications, 1993) p.271
17. R.S. Thomas, 'Suddenly', *Collected Poems*, p.426
18. Thomas Traherne, *Centuries*, (Faith Press, 1960), p.13 and H.M. Margoliouth, Ed. Traherne's *Thanksgivings*, (Oxford, 1958) p.229
19. Kathleen Raine, 'The Return', *Selected Poems*, (Golgonooza Press, 1988), p.97.
20. T.S. Eliot, 'Little Gidding', *Four Quartets*, p.36
21. Ruth Pitter, 'Spectrum', *Lion Christian Poetry Collection*, p.370
22. Philip Larkin, 'Church Going', *Collected Poems*, (Faber and Faber 1988), p.97
23. Philip Larkin, 'An Arundel Tomb', ibid., p.110
24. Alan Ecclestone, *Yes to God*, p.39
25. Evelyn Underhill, quoted in J. Neville Ward, *The Use of Praying*, (Epworth Press, 1967), p.89
26. Anne Sexton, in Alan Ecclestone, *Gather the Fragments*, p.238
27. George Herbert, 'The Flower', *Poems*, p.171
28. Maria Boulding, op. cit., p.42
29. Elizabeth Jennings, 'A Litany for Contrition', *Times and Seasons*, p.37
30. Mother Teresa, *In the silence of the heart*, (SPCK, 1983), p.19.
31. Mother Mary Clare, *Encountering the Depths*, (Darton, Longman and Todd, 1981), p.33, 21
32. Elizabeth Jennings, *Collected Poems*, p.173
33. W.H. Auden, 'In memory of W.B. Yeats', op. cit., (Faber and Faber, 1976), p.198
34. Ephesians 5:20

CHAPTER IV

Pilgrimage

A genuine exodus is full of surprises
(Alan Ecclestone)

Some writers on prayer speak of it as being an adventure. For many of us 'adventure' may be the last thing we want in our prayer. Rather, are we likely to be seeking quiet reassurance and tranquillity. For adventure brings risk and uncertainty, calls us to new and demanding effort. As we look for a renewal of strength and hope through prayer, we are likely to be more concerned with present worries than with looking for future new and unexpected challenges. We want prayer to be a help to us on our spiritual journey and to help us to face the demands of each day; we may find it unsettling to be told that prayer is itself the journey. Alan Ecclestone, in that great exploration of prayer which is his 'Yes to God', writes of prayer as 'the beginning of a long, difficult and surprising journey, by no means the first of such journeys in which men have lost their way and found their hearts failing them.'[1] And he goes on to speak of prayer as a sort of exodus.

A genuine exodus is full of surprises. The kind of engagement in prayer for the life of the world which we contemplate now is bound to be so charged with new versions of old problems and entirely novel difficulties that there may be little to help us in what we have done in the past. We have to learn to live beyond sheer continuity or precedent, to live off the land, to expect to be shown by the Spirit at each stage of the effort what it is that must be attempted now . . . It means learning to let go much in which we have hitherto trusted, attached great importance to and valued rightly at that time . . . To pray for the world of today is to be immersed in a sea of difficulties . . .

Exploration, geographical and spiritual, exposes men and women to new ordeals, and their praying reflects their attempts to meet them. Such souls must face with courage the loss of all the guidelines of familiar features. They must accept the need to let go the things in which they have trusted and face the outlines of a strange benumbing terrifying world.[2]

Here is a country far removed from the quietude of tranquillity we are so earnestly seeking as we bring our daily concerns to God. Yet it is clear that great souls at prayer, those who have mined the depths of prayer, who seem to have found that personal relationship with God which is at the heart of prayer, have experienced a spiritual journey which has taken them into a new country.

They are seeking to say Yes to God from depths hitherto unexplored. Their praying takes on the character of exodus from the known accepted world, though they cherish whatever in it assists devotion to Him they seek. Profoundly committed to their search, they are explorers every bit as adventurous as Columbus and Da Gama. New dimensions of human consciousness that have lain unvisited as yet, new perceptions of the eternal order clothed in time, are apprehended in their praying and compel them to find new words to describe the journey of the soul.[3]

It is instructive to read how often those who have undertaken the spiritual journey deep into the country of prayer refer to a desert experience. For some it is a time when they feel, truly, bereft of God. For others, the attempt to achieve solitude becomes their overriding need. Deserts of the spirit are not places, but are experiences of the mind and soul through which we pass, during which we learn much about the journey of prayer.

The desert is a teacher. It offers an illustration of the danger of prayer. You hope to pass calmly through the prayer country. There are pleasant pauses. You admire spiritual landscapes which fill you with peace. Your itinerary is well planned. A few excursions into fresh territory, but care is taken to provide precise points of reference. And there is a base camp to receive you back into familiar surroundings. You have obviously not taken seriously the sign which said, 'Danger! Prayer'. As soon as you leave the security of the oasis, you find yourself inevitably in the middle of a storm. It is prayer that brutally crosses your path, shaking you, jolting you, disorienting you . . . Prayer invalidates all your previous knowledge, radically questions your experience, and ridicules the books which were indispensable to you . . . It would therefore be advisable to ensure that places of prayer have clear signs with the words: 'Danger! Prayer'.[4]

We may find such warnings unwelcome and off-putting and take the view that they hardly apply to me. Prayer as risk is something we may not warm to at all. We have enough turbulence in our lives, why should we risk more? But Jesus calls us to abundance of life, not stagnation. He wishes us, surely, to experience the joy of finding him and growing in him. Prayer is growth in the spirit and we shall not have that growth unless we are prepared to venture in faith. To venture into the desert is not as outlandish as it may seem.

Deserts, silence, solitudes are not necessarily places but states of mind and heart. These deserts can be found in the midst of the city, and in the every day of our lives. We need only look for them and realize our tremendous need for them. They will be small solitudes, little deserts, tiny pools of silence, but the experience they will bring, if we are disposed to enter them, may be as exultant and as holy as all the deserts of the world, even the one God himself entered. For it is God who makes solitude, deserts and silences holy . . . One of the first steps towards solitude is a departure. Were you to depart to a real desert, you might take a plane, train or car to get there. But we're blind to the 'little departures' which fill our days. These 'little solitudes' are often right behind a door which we can open, or in a little corner where we can stop to look at a tree that somehow has survived the snow and dust of a city street. This too can be a 'point of departure' to a desert, silence, solitude.[5]

We do not stand still on our spiritual journey. We either make progress in faith and hope, much of the time consciously struggling, but with a deepening experience of the love of God, or we lose our way, trackless in the desert or stuck in a cul-de-sac of indifference or frustration. Prayer should be a pilgrimage of the spirit in which we make a journey, but so much of our prayer is more a daily commuting than a pilgrimage. The thing about daily commuting is that you hardly notice the journey. It is all so routine, so expected, that so much is unnoticed or deliberately shut out. God would have us seek him with some effort, with a sense of determination and with a readiness to know the joy of experiencing those perceptive moments en route when we know that God is with us – for we are all called to know the Emmaus road experience: 'Did not our hearts burn within us?' (Luke 24:32).

A pilgrimage takes us into strange, unfamiliar country; there is a goal to reach, and some personal cost and effort is involved, and the way will not always be easy. The journey of the Magi, as reported in St Matthew's Gospel tells us of the end of that pilgrimage, with the wise men, having reached their goal, then setting out to return 'by another way' – changed men with changed routes and changed expectations. Lancelot Andrewes fills in, by way of imagination, something of the background, the difficulties of the journey and contrasts our own reluctance to undertake a pilgrimage of the spirit:

> Many a wide and weary step they made before they could come to say, 'Lo, here we are come', come and at our journey's end . . . the distance of the place . . . many a day's journey . . . all the way waste and desolate . . . exceeding dangerous. It was no summer progress. A cold coming they had of it at this time of the year, the worst time of the year to take a journey. The ways deep, the weather sharp, the days short . . . the very depth of winter. They saw and they came, no sooner saw, but they set out presently. A sign they highly valued his birth, believed some great matter of it, that they took all these pains, made all haste, that they might be there to worship Him with all the possible speed they could. Sorry for nothing so much that they could not be there soon enough. And

we, what should we have done? Our fashion is to see and see again before we stir a foot. Come such a journey at such a time? No, but fairly have put it off till the Spring of the year, till the days longer and the ways fairer and the weather warmer. Our Epiphany would surely have fallen in Easter-week at the soonest. For the distance, desolations, tediousness and the rest, any of them were enough to mar our coming . . . our religion is rather a contemplation than a motion, or stirring to be ought. But when *we* do it, we must be allowed leisure . . . ever coming, never come. We love to make no very great haste. The truth is, we value Him and His birth too slenderly . . . they like enough to leave us behind. Best get us a new Christmas in September; we are not likely to come to Christ at this present.[6]

Our pilgrimage of the spirit is unlikely to have anything like as clear an objective as the journey of the Magi. We live from day to day, we bring to God in our prayers the concerns of each day. Not for us the achievement of the goal; rather are we seeking some experience of growth, a deepening perception of the depth of God's love for us, a growing awareness of his grace at work in the world. It is the agnostic Thomas Hardy who sets the scene for me:

> In the third-class seat sat the journeying boy,
>   And the roof-lamp's oily flame
> Played down on his listless form and face,
> Bewrapt past knowing to what he was going,
>   Or whence he came.
>
> In the band of his hat the journeying boy
>   Had a ticket stuck; and a string
> Around his neck bore the key of his box,
> That twinkled gleams of the lamp's sad beams
>   Like a living thing.
>
> What past can be yours, O journeying boy
>   Towards a world unknown,
> Who calmly, as if incurious quite
> On all at stake, can undertake
>   This plunge alone?

> Knows your soul a sphere, O journeying boy,
>   Our rude realms far above.
> Whence with spacious vision you mark and mete
> This region of sin that you find you in,
>   But are not of?[7]

I see myself as the journeying boy, seeking a destination. I set out in the dark and ask that there may be light upon my path. One might have expected Hardy to have asked of the future, but his question is 'What past can be yours?'. We bring to our prayers our past and our present and we seek that sphere whence we may be given spacious vision to be relieved of the burden of the past and strengthened to meet the challenge of the present and the future. There is so much in our past we need to break free of; and we hope so much that we can be enabled to rise above those things in the present that keep us from the freedom of the spirit which is of the love of God. Yet the idea of prayer as pilgrimage can cause uncertainty; uncertain the goal and the way and uncertain too, the intention. That we should seek to be challenged and changed through prayer is precisely one context of praying 'Thy will be done', but it is a context that can be difficult to accept. Much easier to offer our petitions to God than to offer ourselves. But we are always searching are we not?

> What are our lives but harbours
> we are continually setting out
> from, airports at which we touch
> down and remain in too briefly
> to recognize what it is they remind
> us of?[8]

Prayer is a journey inwards in which we have to find out about ourselves and about God and it is this journey inwards which is so difficult and which can seem so self-indulgent. Praying hard for others is a form of self-giving; but what am I doing for others if I set out on a pilgrimage which is the exploration of self? One answer is that the only way to true self-giving is by offering ourselves to God. Our pilgrimage in prayer has to be, not the discovery of self, but the setting aside of self. 'The Kingdom of God', said Jesus, 'is within you'.

If we cannot find the kingdom of God within us, if we cannot meet God within, in the very depth of ourselves, our chances of meeting him outside ourselves are very remote. When Gagarin came back from space and made his remarkable statement that he never saw God in heaven, a priest in Moscow remarked, 'If you have not seen him on earth, you will never see him in heaven.' This is also true of what I am speaking about. If we cannot find a contact with God under our own skin, as it were, in this very small world in which I am, then the chances are very slight that even if I meet him face to face, I will recognize him. St John Chrysostom said, 'Find the door of your heart, and discover it is the door of the kingdom of God.' So it is inward we must turn, and not outward – but inward in a very special way. I am not saying that we must become introspective. I don't mean that we must go inward in the way one does in psychoanalysis or psychology. It is not a journey into *my own* inwardness; it is a journey *through* my own self, in order to emerge from the deepest level of self into the place where he is, the point at which God and I meet.[9]

The way of prayer, the journey inward, is a continuing journey, for there are always things to find out about God and about ourselves, and it must always be a journey forward:

Friend, I have lost the way.
The way leads on.
Is there another way?
The way is one.
I must retrace the track.
It's lost and gone.
Back, I must travel back!
None goes there, none.
Then I'll make here my place.
(The road runs on)

53

Stand still and set my face.
(The road leaps on),
Stay here, for ever stay.
None stays here, none.
I cannot find the way.
The way leads on.
Oh places I have passed!
That journey's done.
And what will come at last?
The way leads on.[10]

This sounds as though we are being invited to undertake a never-ending journey in which the objective is just to keep going. There are indeed times when prayer feels like that, times, too, when, as a walker trudges mechanically to reach the summit or the next bend in the road, we keep going with our prayers though they may be uninspired or lifeless. The point about a pilgrimage is that we do indeed keep going; we must expect the dreary stretches. But there is another sort of expectation in a pilgrimage; an expectation of moments of awareness that transform perception. Kathleen Raine would have us see ourselves walking in the steps of the saints:

Those whose faces are turned always to the sun's rising
See the living light on its path approaching
As, over the glittering sea where in tide's rising and falling
The sea-beasts bask, on the Isles of Farne
Aidan and Cuthbert saw God's feet walking
Each day towards all who on the world's shores await his coming.
There we too, hand in hand, have received the unending morning.[11]

We don't have to go to a holy place to receive 'the unending morning'. Praying in faith opens our eyes to the coming of God to us. But the pilgrimage of prayer, the journey inwards, is not all Lindisfarne light; we seem, often enough, to perceive more of God's absence than his presence. The inward search might seem to take us further away God.

Was the pilgrimage
I made to come to my own
self, to learn that in times
like these and for one like me
God will never be plain and
out there, but dark rather and
inexplicable, as though he were in here?[12]

And not only darkness and inexplicability lurk on the way, but loneliness:

A pen appeared, and the god said:
'Write what it is to be
man.' And my hand hovered
long over the bare page,

until there, like footprints
of the lost traveller, letters
took shape on the page's
blankness, and I spelled out

the word 'lonely'. And my hand moved
to erase it; but the voices
of all those waiting at life's
window cried out loud: 'It is true.'[13]

Chaucer's Canterbury Pilgrims were a jolly lot; the personal pilgrimage of the spirit is a very different venture. There are no regular landmarks on this journey and but little opportunity to share our deepest concerns with others. Even that great poet of joy and felicity, George Herbert, could find the going exceedingly wearisome:

I travelled on, seeing the hill, where lay
My expectation.
A long it was and weary way.
The gloomy cave of Desperation
I left on th'one, and on the other side
The rock of Pride.[14]

55

If he could find it so difficult, where does that leave us? It leaves us in the hand of God. The fact that we pray at all is evidence of the God who is within us. Recognizing and accepting our dependence upon God is both where we start and is the journey. There is no other. So often, it is what we are seeking, our own imposed vision of the objectives of prayer, which is wrong. It is not that God gives us nothing, it is rather that we are not sufficiently perceptive of what he does give us. We are so intent upon getting to the centre of the maze, as Edwin Muir puts it, that we ignore our God who is with us on the way:

> Did we come here, drawn by some fatal thing,
> Fly from eternity's immaculate bow
> Straight to the heart of time's great turning ring,
> That we might win the prize that took us so?
> Was it some ordinary sight, a flower,
> The white wave falling, falling upon the shore,
> The blue of the sky, the grasses' waving green?
>
> Or was it one sole thing, a certain door
> Set in a wall, a half-conjectured scene
> Of men and women moving as in a play,
> A turn in the winding road, a distant tower,
> A corner of a field, a single place
> Apart, a single house, a single tree,
> A look upon one half-averted face
> That has been once, or is, or is to be?
>
> We hurried here for some such thing and now
> Wander the countless roads to seek our prize,
> That far within the maze serenely lies,
> While all around each trivial shape exclaims:
> 'Here is your jewel; this is your longed for day',
> And we forget, lost in the countless names.[15]

What we are granted by God in our pilgrimage, is not the final vision in which we can rest, knowing that we have arrived. It may be a glimpse of the vision, something yet to be attained, as with Moses and the promised land. But the joy of the pilgrimage is an acceptance of the gift of a new way of seeing. The God who walks with us does not clear the way of obstacles, does not spirit us around dark and threatening places. He is with us. The recognition that he is with us comes, often enough, with a new way of seeing, a new way of understanding and accepting. Sometimes the new way of seeing is retrospective and tardy on our part – looking back we are able to see something of a pattern, something of God's grace at work in our lives. The answer to prayer can come, not as a change in circumstances, through the intervention of God, but in the strength we are given, whatever the odds, in the reassurance in which we come to know that we are never separated from God's love, and in a deepening of trust in him. Our journey of the spirit in prayer is a search for God in which we must set aside preconceived notions of God and struggle with new ways of perceiving him. Elizabeth Jennings gives us a clue as to what this means when she is writing about Edward Thomas, a poet who gave much to her and of whom she wanted to know more.

> I have looked about for you many times,
> Mostly in woods or down quiet roads,
> Often in birds whose question-times
> Sound like the echo of your moods
>
> When sombre. I've not found you yet
> In day sounds or dream-threaded night
> You watched through, tired-eyed. I set
> Such places by, finding no sight
>
> Of you in this strange hunt. I turn
> Back to your words. You do not haunt
> Them either. Suddenly I learn
> Your art of being reticent,
>
> Of leaving birds, trees, hills alone.
> You left no spirit in any place
> Or spoors of yours where you had gone.
> Yet, though there is no print or trace

Of you, I *see* a different way,
As if your writing were a shine
Upon cool suns, your words the play
Of stars with water, your dark – mine.[16]

Searching for God in our prayers is rather like Elizabeth
Jennings' hunt for Edward Thomas. We want to feel that we
possess him, which means bringing him down to our level. But
God will not be confined within the limits of our perception; it is
our perception which must be extended, transformed, so that we
may become aware of him in different ways. 'Though there is no
print or trace of him, we see in a different way'. We find we have
been looking for the wrong thing in the wrong way, our
perception dimmed by the constraints we put upon our prayers. It
is when we find our freedom in prayer that we shall know that we
are walking in the ways of God. The word, 'Father', in our prayers
must become a word of recognition just as much as a word of
appeal. When we can say that word in recognition of the God
who is with us, then we have our freedom as children of God, a
freedom to which Christ the Way calls us.

W.H. Auden in his Christmas Oratorio, 'For the Time Being',
has the three wise men say:

To discover how to be human now
Is the reason we follow the star.[17]

Theirs was a journey of self-discovery culminating in the finding
of the Christ-child. They were discovering how to be open to the
world's possibilities; how to offer themselves to the God who
comes in weakness; discovering how to find in uncertainty and
vulnerability the God who calls to a greater faith and a surer trust.
Each wise man, in Auden's play, was walking his own path of self-
discovery: how to be truthful, how to be living, how to be loving.
In our prayers, as we open ourselves to the God who is near, we are
challenged by truth, by life, by love. The pilgrimage of prayer takes
us deeper into each of these territories. We learn more and more of
the truth of ourselves, of the false gods in our lives, of our need for

others, of our powerlessness in the great issues which concern us and of our misuse of power in those issues we can influence. We learn more about God, who calls us to walk the way of the Cross. We shall want to pray to be 'living now', to experience the demands of a God who calls us in love to know the pain and the joy of the world, a broken world, yet one in which the power of love speaks through the brokenness, a world in which there is still room for thanksgiving, day by day. We need, says Alan Ecclestone, to 'compile our own Benedicite'.[18] To do that we must be observant of the ways in which the world is being remade. 'We are to pray . . . as those . . . who grow in wonder and delight at the vast context of God's action. We are to pray, no matter how still our bodies, as those who are sustained by the great tidal wave of His oncoming Kingdom. We are to pray, no matter how silent our lips, as those who join the dawn-chorus of a new creation.'[19] And we shall want to pray to be loving now, to know the love which comes from the will to be self-giving, the love which seeks to understand and to heal, not to possess. These are the paths of discovery we walk in our prayers as we find what it means to be 'human now'. It is the road upon which we discover that 'without our knowledge, love has used our weakness as a guard and guide',[20] in which we find that 'lonely we were though never left alone'.[21]

This chapter started with expressions of reservation about the notion of adventure in prayer and hazarded the thought that the search in prayer for most of us is for reassurance rather than challenge. But if there is to be any growth as we pray, any spiritual development, we shall find ourselves following a way of discovery, which is itself an adventure. It may be a very tortuous and uncertain way but Christ who is the Way calls us to walk with him.

He is the Way.
Follow Him through the Land of Unlikeness;
You will see rare beasts, and have unique adventures.

He is the Truth.
Seek Him in the Kingdom of Anxiety;
You will come to a great city that has expected your return for years.

He is the Life.
Love Him in the World of the Flesh;
And at your marriage all its occasions shall dance for joy.[22]

Sources

1. Alan Ecclestone, *Yes to God*, p.71
2. Ibid., p.71
3. Ibid., p.31
4. Allessandro Pronzato, *Meditations on the Sand*, (St Paul Publications, 1982), p.9
5. Catherine de Hueck Doherty, *Poustinia: Christian Spirituality of the East for Western Man*, (Ave Maria Press, 1975), p.21
6. Lancelot Andrewes, Sermon preached before the King at Whitehall, Christmas Day 1622
7. Thomas Hardy, 'Midnight on the Great Western', *Collected Poems*, (Macmillan, 1930), p.483
8. R.S. Thomas, 'Somewhere', *Collected Poems*, p.293
9. Anthony Bloom (Metropolitan Anthony of Sourozh), *School for Prayer*, (Darton, Longman and Todd, 1989), p.49
10. Edwin Muir, 'The Way', *Collected Poems*, p.166
11. Kathleen Raine, 'The Holy Isles', *Selected Poems*, p.149
12. R.S. Thomas, 'Pilgrimages', *Collected Poems*, p.364
13. R.S. Thomas, 'The Word', ibid., p.265
14. George Herbert, 'The Pilgrimage', *The English Poems of George Herbert*, p.151
15. Edwin Muir, 'The Prize', *Collected Poems*, p.111
16. Elizabeth Jennings, 'For Edward Thomas', *Collected Poems*, p.161
17. W.H. Auden, 'For the Time Being', *Collected Poems*, p.286
18. Alan Ecclestone, op. cit., p.130
19. Ibid., p.125
20. W.H. Auden, 'For the Time Being', op. cit., p.295
21. Ibid., p.294
22. Ibid., p.308

CHAPTER V

Relationships

Love is proved in the letting go
(C. Day Lewis)

We find ourselves and we come to know ourselves in our relationships with others. We come to know ourselves more fully in our relationships with God. These two statements, especially the second, are truths that are forgotten and denied in our modern culture. In the battle between the two conflicting modern ideologies, the cult of the individual and subjection to the collective, the paramount truths of personhood have become diminished. The emphasis is upon empowerment – of the individual or the collective – not upon openness to others, which, for the Christian, must be the unconditional acceptance of another person as the child of God. Fulfilment in our personal lives comes, not through possession or manipulation of others, nor through a wary distancing of ourselves in the name of independence, but in the recognition of the worth and value of the other person. Our own worth and value are reflected in the way in which we work out that recognition, not in the pursuit of self. Much of our prayer is about relationships; about our concerns for others, about the joy we are given through friends and family, about the pain we feel for others or in ourselves when others let us down. We bring our relationships to God in our prayers, not only our very personal encounters and dependencies, but also those relationships which reflect our wider concerns for the world in which we live and for the community which shapes us. In our prayers we deepen our relationships, for 'prayer is nothing if not a personal act of engagement with another.'[1] When we pray, we are not merely presenting our concerns to God, we are inviting him to give us a better understanding of others, to help us to enrich lives, both the lives of others and our own. We are seeking to open up ourselves to his guidance so that we may be more aware of how we depend upon others for our enrichment. 'A self which does not receive its character and direction from the eternal is already lost.'[2]

The concerns of our personal relationships weigh heavily and are sometimes too much for us. Then the solace of prayer is sought in a coming close to God, in relief from the burdens we carry because of others. There is a longing then for escape of a sort:

> Away, away...
> To the silent wilderness
> Where the soul need not repress
> Its music, lest it should not find
> An echo in another's mind.[3]

Prayer is not a silent wilderness, but it does offer a place where we need not repress the music of our soul; not singing to ourselves, but allowing God to sing in us and to help us to express our deepest fears and our most worrying anxieties. It is where we are given strength to endure them.

Human relationships lead us into prayer, and not always because of the weight of our care. Our relationships test us and grieve us and they also give us great joy. Sometimes they break us and we have nowhere to go except to God for relief and help. Sometimes it is in chance encounters, a quick passing moment, or in the fleetest experience of the closeness of a loving relationship that we are granted something of a vision of the love of God. We are helped in those moments towards prayer, for prayer is an opening of our eyes, not just a closing of our eyes and folding of our hands.

> There are in our existence spots of time,
> That with distinct pre-eminence retain
> A renovating virtue...

A virtue, by which pleasure is enhanced,
That penetrates, enables us to mount,
When high, more high, and lifts us up when fallen . . .
Such moments are scattered everywhere.[4]

Wordsworth found such 'spots of time', moments of awareness, times when he was 'surprised by joy',[5] especially in his reflections upon his childhood. Prayer, too, offers a 'renovating virtue', times of healing and renewal in our lives. It is these, surely, we are seeking when we pray. There are two sets of interaction at work when we pray – the interaction of the temporal and the eternal, and the interaction of human lives. When I pray for others, or for myself, in relation to others, I am entering into their lives, sharing to some extent their joy and sorrow, their weakness and vulnerability, their loneliness or rejection. This is the act of engagement at the heart of personal prayer. And the interaction of the temporal and the eternal comes as the mystery of the grace of God at work in the ways of both suffering and renewal. They come, these spots of time, as moments of transformation from our prayers. We may not often recognize them or react to them consciously, but they enter into our relationships. They give us changed perceptions and changed understanding; they heighten our personal joys; they do not dispel the darkness we have to endure but confirm that we are not alone in that darkness.

'Such moments are scattered everywhere', said Wordsworth. How may we find them, hold on to them, these evidences of the grace of God? A few years ago, the playwright Dennis Potter was interviewed on television by Melvyn Bragg. He knew that he had but a short time to live; the interview had to be interrupted from time to time while he dosed himself against the pain of cancer. That interview made a telling impression upon very many people because of the courage of the man. One striking thing that Dennis Potter said was that the approach of death had changed his way of looking at things, had changed his appreciation and his experience of his relationships with the world. 'Things are both more trivial than they ever were', he said, 'and more important than they ever were. And the difference between the trivial and the important doesn't seem to matter. But the **nowness** of everything is **absolutely wondrous** . . . there's no way of telling you; you have to experience it. But the **glory** of it, the comfort of it, the reassurance! The fact is that if you see the present tense, **boy** do you see it, and **boy** can you celebrate it!' The sacrament of the present moment comes as an experience of the glory of God, in the seemingly trivial, in the high points of shared joy, in the dark ways of suffering. The great paradox of the Christian religion is that God's glory is made manifest in the passion of Jesus. 'Father, the hour has come,' Jesus said, 'glorify thy Son, that thy Son may glorify thee.'[6] That was in the upper room, before Jesus walked out into the night and into the garden of Gethsemane. If prayer is a walking with God, and not just a talking to God, we shall find him in all things and especially we shall find him in the relationships that make up our lives. Even in the most ordinary of circumstances there can be an experience of 'nowness', of what I would call the experience of God's presence in, and through, ordinary, everyday things.

> There's something religious in the way we sit
> At the tea table, a tidy family of three.
> You, my love, slicing the bread and butter, and she,
> The red-cheeked tot a smear of blackberry jam, and me . . .
> A new creation is established, a true presence.
> And talking to each other, breaking words over food
> Is somehow different to customary chatting.[7]

We have all felt such occasions of 'new creation', from time to time, without perhaps fully acknowledging them and, even if we have acknowledged them, we may not have drawn them into our prayers, giving thanks for the precious wonder of awareness and reflecting upon the richness of relationships illuminated by love. We need a sense of wonder in our prayers; wonder that is reverence and awe before the transcendent God and wonder that is also earthed, literally, in the mundane, yet astonishing, magic of being.

But we are wary, are we not, of moving beyond the level of 'customary chatting'? And to establish a 'true presence' might seem rather remote from our common experience of a family meal, whether rushed and chaotic or of routine ordinariness and sameness. In any case, it is the raw edges of life which perplex and hurt us, make us wary of openness. We become well-schooled in the art of building protective walls to shield us from too close an involvement with others. Only with very few can we share the closeness that is complete trust. Even in our prayers, much as we seek honesty and self-offering, we all too often hold back something of ourselves. Intercession can become a barrier to self-offering; we offer others to God and our anxieties and fears, but we hold back ourselves. Much as we would like to feel within ourselves something of the reality of the love of God, we cannot grasp the reality of the mystery of that love. How can we be upheld by God's love when, for so much of our lives, we feel a sense of separation, of loneliness? Fully to grasp the mystery is beyond us, but we are given some insights into the wonder of God's love for us as we experience the demands, the power, and the vulnerability, of human love. C. Day Lewis wrote a poem for Sean, his first-born son, which gives a glimpse of the demands, the risks, of love:

> It is eighteen years ago, almost to the day –
> A sunny day with leaves just turning,
> The touch-lines new-ruled – since I watched you play
> Your first game of football, then, like a satellite
> Wrenched from its orbit, go drifting away
>
> Behind a scatter of boys. I can see
> You walking away from me towards the school
> With the pathos of a half-fledged thing set free
> Into a wilderness, the gait of one
> Who finds no path where the path should be.

That hesitant figure, eddying away
Like a winged seed loosened from its parent stem,
Has something I never quite grasp to convey
About nature's give-and-take – the small, the scorching
Ordeals which fire one's irresolute clay.

I have had worse partings, but none that so
Gnaws at my mind still. Perhaps it is roughly
Saying what God alone could perfectly show –
How selfhood begins with a walking away,
And love is proved in the letting go.[8]

The poem presents us with a poignant picture of something we have all experienced or observed – the bitter-sweet business of growing up, the pain of parting, the fears that gnaw as one's children take independence and distance themselves in their own world. 'Selfhood begins with a walking away.' To claim and to experience freedom always involves a walking away from ties of one sort or another, and also a walking away into the unknown. God grants us freedom, which we exercise by distancing ourselves from him, all too often. Yet, without freedom, it would not be a relationship in love. We can perceive only dimly what Day Lewis states so boldly – that his experience with his own boy's growing up is 'roughly saying what God alone could perfectly show.'

When we come before God in our prayers we do not stand before a God who coerces and compels, but we open ourselves to a God who wills us by his love. And when we bring before God the needs of others, when we express before him our anguish for those whose sufferings we share and would so wish to take upon ourselves, we must seek in our prayers that comfort and reassurance which comes from 'letting go', by having trust and faith that we really can 'cast our burden upon the Lord and he will sustain us.'[9] This is not a matter of leaving our problems with (and to) God whilst we get on with the rest of our lives, any more than Day Lewis's 'letting go' was a matter of simply allowing his son to walk out of his life. The son's walking away did not lessen the bond of love, did not weaken the caring concern of the father.

In bringing our deepest needs before God in prayer we must be willing to let go in the assurance of the strength of his love. Likewise, when we bring our failings to God, when we have badly let down someone we love, or have been unfair and hurtful to others, and we ask for God's forgiveness, then, having truly felt our shame and remorse, we must let go and not continually condemn ourselves or torture ourselves with self-recrimination.

When we share our love with another person, there are no barriers; so it is also between ourselves and God. Prayer is acceptance and growth of a relationship without barriers and without separation, and we find, as we grow in our prayer, that it is the certainty of that relationship which upholds us and those for whom we pray. When we have the love of another person we know that we draw, not just comfort and reassurance from the dependability, the constancy, of that person's love, but we draw strength also, a strength which enables and empowers. In that strength we find resolution and hope, we find the redeeming power of love. So it is with the love of God, and finding that love, coming to know it as the transforming centre of our being is the true answer to our prayer. St Paul talks about rejoicing in sufferings, which will be somewhat beyond us; it is enough, at times, to be able to endure without being overcome. But the truth that Paul is expressing is valid for all who know the redeeming power of love, whether that love is human or divine. To come to know the experience of the love of God is to be given something of a transforming presence which changes our lives. Some of St Paul's other words become a reality: 'suffering produces endurance, and endurance produces character, and character produces hope, and hope does not disappoint us because God's love has been poured into our hearts.'[10] Hope gives resolution and courage and is the enemy of cynicism, which is the rot in so much of our modern society. Love brings hope and hope is found, not in shallow optimism or in blinkered avoidance of reality, nor in stoical endurance, but in the experience of the transforming quality of goodness.

By a windrowed field she made me stop.
'I love it – finding you one of these,'
She said; and I watched her tenderly stoop
Towards a sprig of shy heartsease
Among the ruined crop.

'Oh but look, it is everywhere!'
Stubble and flint and sodden tresses
Of hay were a prospect of despair:
But a myriad infant heartsease faces
Pensively eyed us there.

Long enough had I found that flower
Little more common than what it is named for –
A chance-come solace amid earth's sour
Failures, a minute joy that bloomed for
Its brief, precocious hour.

No marvel that she, who gives me peace
Wherein my shortening days redouble
Their yield, could magically produce
From all that harshness of flint and stubble
Whole acres of heartsease.[11]

It is precisely in the hope we are given in our living human relationships that we find heartsease amid 'the harshness of flint and stubble.' So it is also in prayer that we are given relief and refreshment and the strength to face new challenges and to accept continuing burdens. Such easements of the heart come through a closeness that is inarticulate yet powerful, the closeness that we experience in the deepest of human relationships and in our coming to God.

Your hands lie open in the long fresh grass –
The finger points look through like rosy blooms:
Your eyes smile peace. The pasture gleams and glooms
'Neath billowing skies that scatter and amass.
All round our nest, far as the eye can pass,
Are golden kingcup-fields with silver edge
Where the cow-parsley skirts the hawthorn-hedge.

'Tis visible silence, still as the hour-glass.
Deep in the sun-searched growths the dragon-fly
Hangs like a blue thread loosened from the sky:-
So this winged hour is dropped to us from above.
Oh! clasp we to our hearts, for deathless dower,
This close-companioned inarticulate hour
When two-fold silence was the song of love.[12]

If only our prayers, and our human relationships, were made up of a continual enjoyment and exploration of 'close-companioned inarticulate hours'! But it is not so. The Psalms fairly reflect the whole gamut of human emotions and bring them before God in prayer. In some of them there is a raging against God and against enemies and supposed friends; there is the agony of the breakdown of trust. It is in the very depths of despair that the psalmist comes before God; his prayers reflect the bitter reality of isolation, rejection, betrayal. Where, then, is the consolation of heartsease, the reassurance of trust, the stimulus of hope? 'Out of the deep have I called unto thee O Lord.'[13] Here is the cry that we are familiar with, the substance of so much of our prayer. 'For my soul is full of trouble: and my life draweth nigh unto hell. I have been even as a man that hath no strength.'[14] It is in the extremity of personal betrayal that David prays to the Lord. 'Hear my prayer, O God: and hide not thyself from my petition. My heart is disquieted within me: and the fear of death is fallen upon me. For it is not an open enemy that hath done me this dishonour: for then I could have borne it. But it was even thou, my companion: my guide and my own familiar friend.'[15] Here is the breakdown of human relationship and a turning to God for healing and for restoration of trust. At such times we may well feel that God has left us. We may find it difficult to echo the apparent confidence of David when he says, 'As for me, I will call upon God: and the Lord shall save me. In the evening and in the morning, and at noonday I will pray, and that instantly; and he shall hear my voice.'[16] Our experience is, so very often, that in spite of constant, urgent prayer, we cannot feel that the Lord has heard our voice, and we seem far from being saved by him. Our despair and desolation in the breakdown of a human relationship, in experiencing some great pain and hurt in our lives, is mirrored in a desolate loss of God. The gap we are endeavouring to bridge through our prayers is a chasm of emptiness and we feel utterly lost.

Where is the God of love and compassion, **where is** the abundance of life that Jesus said he comes to give us? How can we find God in the desolation and separation and pain? I find clues to some answers to this question in a tough, uncompromising poem by R.S. Thomas:

> Not as in the old days I pray,
> God. My life is not what it was.
>   . . . once I would have asked
> healing.
> . . . I would have knelt
> long, wrestling with you, wearing
> you down. Hear my prayer, Lord, hear
> my prayer.
>   It begins to appear
> this is not what prayer is about.
>   I begin to recognize
> you anew . . .
> There are questions we are the solution
> to, others whose echoes we must expand
> to contain. Circular as our way
> is, it leads not back to that snake-haunted
> garden, but onward to the tall city
> of glass that is the laboratory of the spirit.[17]

What is that 'tall city of glass', the 'laboratory of the spirit that Thomas speaks of? It can be a chilling metaphor, off-putting in its clinical coldness. For laboratories can be unwelcoming in their very impersonality, strange, unreal places where all is foreign and unknown. What could such a place have to do with prayer? A laboratory can, indeed, be a strange, forbidding place, a home only for the initiated, but the essence of a laboratory is that it is a place of searching. It is a place where truth is sought and confirmed, where new worlds are entered into, strange and wonderful worlds, a place where the boundaries of experience are extended and the mind stretched; where the unfamiliar is brought into a recognisable pattern; a place where single-minded service of the truth prevails in the faith that those who seek shall find; a place of engagement. I find here helpful analogies to the process of prayer. Engagement in prayer, which is engagement in the world, calls us into growth in the spirit, where we advance beyond calling to the Lord as though he were deaf and we find a new recognition of God, the God who calls us into a richer world of spiritual experience, the God who would have us explore the immensities of his demanding love. This is the I-Thou relationship come to life, as when, in a human relationship, communication between individuals grows into understanding and commitment, into the mutual self-giving of love.

Julian of Norwich wrote: 'God looks on us with love and wants to make us his partners in good deeds.'[18] There is both a promise and a challenge here. The promise is that of closer understanding and of realizing and accepting that we have a God-given purpose which is based upon his love for us. The challenge is that of accepting that God works in us and through us and depends upon us; we must therefore be constant in our readiness to pray, to be open to him. The challenge of partnership is that we move beyond prayer as a beating upon a door which only occasionally seems to open, to a readiness to perceive God in all things. 'Prayer,' says Julian, 'is the proper understanding of the fullness of joy that is to be; an understanding which comes from deep desire and sure trust.'[19] Partnership based upon longing for closeness and trust in dependability is what we seek and find in our most rewarding and fulfilling human relationships. It is what we seek and find in our most rewarding prayer.

In spite of, and because of, the cult of the individual which pervades so much of our culture, it is the fear of being alone, the hopelessness of separation, the desperation of the lack of love, which makes a prison of self. And the fear of separation casts its shadow across even the most fulfilling, the most loving, of relationships. How can one face up to, and accept, the loss of an essential part of oneself when such a relationship is broken, by whatever cause? There are fears that present happiness, present enjoyment, may be fleeting, that the certainties of the present may be lost, that the shine on shared joy and shared love may become tarnished.

> We kissed at the barrier; and passing through
> She left me, and moment by moment got
> Smaller and smaller, until to my view
>   She was but a spot;
>
> A wee white spot of muslin fluff
> That down the diminishing platform bore
> Through hustling crowds of gentle and rough
>   To the carriage door.
>
> Under the lamplight's fitful glowers,
> Behind dark groups from far and near,
> Whose interests were far apart from ours,
>   She would disappear,
>
> Then show again, till I ceased to see
> That flexible form, that nebulous white;
> And she who was more than my life to me
>   Had vanished quite . . .
>
> We have penned new plans since that fair fond day,
> And in season she will appear again –
> Perhaps in the same soft white array –
>   But never as then!
>
> – 'And why, young man, must eternally fly
> A joy you'll repeat, if you love her well?'
> – O friend, nought happens twice thus; why,
>   I cannot tell.[20]

The preciousness of the present moment confirms the vulnerability of our relationships. Trying vainly to recreate the joy

of a treasured, remembered, moment is one thing; facing up to
the fear of separation is another. Harold Monro's plaintive plea
finds its echo in all of us at some time or another:

> Is then, nothing safe?
> Can we not find
> Some everlasting life
> In our one mind?[21]

For some, the fear is of a final irrevocable separation:

> I cannot find a way
> Through love and through;
> I cannot reach beyond
> Body, to you.
> When you or I must go
> Down evermore,
> There'll be no more to say
> – But a locked door.[22]

How does one live with the 'locked door', whether caused by
the final separation of death or by the complete severance of a
relationship because there is no more trust? How can one find, in
prayer, a way through; how can one find the courage to endure,
the strength of hope? There are times in our prayers when God
himself seems to be shut away behind a locked door and we feel
utterly alone. As Jeremiah put it: 'Thou hast wrapped thyself with
a cloud so that no prayer can pass through.'[23] It is difficult at such
times to gain comfort from memories of past blessings; our needs
are in the present and cry out to be met. It is hard indeed to
endure the gulf of separation from one whom you love or to feel
ignored by one whom you trust. As with a human person, so with
our feelings about God. One message that is offered is: 'live
through, let yourself be broken open or ignored by God. Above all
trust',[24] and this may seem a counsel of despair. And yet, the more
we offer ourself in prayers of trust, seeking only to trust, to have
faith, even in emptiness, the surer becomes the conviction that
walking through the darkness is a walk with God; it is through the

separation and the desolation that we find ourselves coming to a depth of understanding of the glory of God, that we are able to offer him ourselves in true thanksgiving.

> We give thanks for St Thomas
> All we who have known
> The darkness of disbelief,
> The hollowness at the heart of Christmas,
> The intolerable emptiness of Easter,
> The grief of separation.
>
> With Thy great mercy Thou dost enfold us,
> The waverers, the aliens, who stood apart, alone.
> For the impoverishment of our barren years
> Thou wilt atone.
>
> Now with the faithful company we bring,
> From depths of thankfulness
> Our adoration
> To Thee,
> O, Christ, our King.[25]

We know that human relationships that look to feed only on undisturbed contentment untroubled by adversity, are likely to be unfulfilled, to lack the deeper understanding which comes when there is a sharing of pain and vulnerability. This is not a matter of trying to glorify suffering and weakness, nor of striving for martyrdom. It is a realistic acceptance of the world as it is, a world of joy and woe, a world in which love and faith are tested, a world in which sometimes the pain is too much and despair and bitterness take over. But a world, also, in which there are constant renewals and remakings, in which love breaks through, again and again, bringing its blessings of hope and, yes, of joy.

> One foot in Eden still, I stand
> And look across the other land.
> The world's great day is growing late,
> Yet strange these fields that we have planted
> So long with crops of love and hate.

Time's handiworks by time are haunted,
And nothing now can separate
The corn and tares compactly grown.
The armorial weed in stillness bound
About the stalk; these are our own.
Evil and good stand thick around
In the fields of charity and sin
Where we shall lead our harvest in.

Yet still from Eden springs the root
As clean as on the starting day.
Time takes the foliage and the fruit
And burns the archetypal leaf
To shapes of terror and of grief
Scattered along the winter way.
But famished field and blackened tree
Bear flowers in Eden never known.
Blossoms of grief and charity
Bloom in these darkened fields alone.
What had Eden ever to say
Of hope and faith and pity and love
Until was buried all its day
And memory found its treasure trove?
Strange blessings never in Paradise
Fall from these beclouded skies.[26]

Learning about 'blossoms of grief and charity that bloom in
darkened fields' is an essential part of the business of prayer, as it
is of living. They are given to us, not to brood over, but to teach
us the ways of love, that hard road in which we find ourselves and
find our joy in God. To experience the power of love in
forgiveness is to know renewal. So much brokenness in human
lives comes from lack of a forgiving spirit, which is a denial of
love. So much in our lives is the struggle with regret which stops
short of forgiveness, both on our part and on the part of others. In
our prayers we struggle with the pressures of regret. One part of us
reaches out for the forgiveness of God and asks that we may truly
know in our hearts that our prayer for forgiveness has been

answered. The other part of us that wishes to right a wrong, to re-establish a relationship, may stop short of granting forgiveness or may come up against the blank wall of another's unforgiving spirit. We have all felt:

> How simple is my burden every day
>> Now you have died, till I am also dead.
> The words, 'Forgive me', that I could not say,
>> The words, 'I am sorry', that you might have said.[27]

It's the little things that bother us, sometimes torture us, in our relationships; the little things that sometimes gnaw away at our lives. We justify our actions, or lack of action, and yet do not dispose of our guilt as we remember our lack of charity.

> She kept an antique shop – or it kept her.
> Among Apostle spoons and Bristol glass,
> The faded silks, the heavy furniture,
> She watched her own reflections in the brass
> Salvers and silver bowls, as if to prove
> Polish was all, there was no need of love.

> And I remember how I once refused
> To go out with her, since I was afraid.
> It was perhaps a wish not to be used
> Like antique objects. Though she never said
> That she was hurt, I could still feel the guilt
> Of that refusal, guessing how she felt.

> Later, too frail to keep a shop, she put
> All her best things in one long narrow room.
> The place smelt old, of things too long kept shut,
> The smell of absences where shadows come
> That can't be polished. There was nothing then
> To give her own reflection back again.

And when she died I felt no grief at all,
Only the guilt of what I had once refused.
I walked into her room among the tall
Sideboards and cupboards – things she never used
But needed; and no finger marks were there,
Only the new dust falling through the air.[28]

In prayer, we offer our sincere, remorseful regrets upon an altar where they are consumed by the flames of God's forgiving love and we are given that newness of life promised by Christ. But there are times when our guilt will not go away and we carry it with us, distorting our lives, for we cannot forgive ourselves. In so doing, we show our lack of trust in God. Then it is we should remember Julian of Norwich:

If God forgives, who are we to withhold forgiveness from ourselves? As by his courtesy God forgives our sins when we repent, even so he wills that we should forgive our sin and so give up senseless worrying and faithless fear. Nor does he will that we should busy ourselves with too much self-accusation; nor is it his will that we should despise ourselves. But he wills that we should quickly turn to him.[29]

We especially need the assurance of forgiveness when we can no longer re-establish a relationship because the final separation of death has intervened. We must pray then for the gift of God which is a quiet spirit of understanding that 'all shall be well, and all manner of things shall be well.'

Thou hast come safe to port
    I still at sea,
The light is on thy head,
    Darkness in me.

Pluck thou in heaven's field
    Violet and rose,
While I strew flowers that will thy vigil keep
Where thou dost sleep,
Love, in thy last repose.[30]

Sources

1. Alan Ecclestone, *Yes to God*, p.106
2. Ibid., p.107
3. P.B. Shelley, 'The Invitation', *The Oxford Book of English Verse*, (Oxford, 1939), p.716
4. William Wordsworth, The Prelude, Book XII, *The Poetical Works*, (Oxford, 1939), p.737
5. Miscellaneous Sonnet, XXVII, ibid., p.257
6. John 17:1
7. Bobi Jones, 'Having our Tea', *Lion Christian Poetry*, p.429
8. C. Day Lewis, 'Walking Away', *Complete Poems*, (Sinclair-Stevenson, 1992), p.546
9. Psalm 55:22
10. Romans 5:4
11. C. Day Lewis, The Upland Field, op. cit., p.554.
12. D.G. Rossetti, 'The House of Life', *Love*, Ed. Walter de la Mare, (Faber and Faber, 1953), p.394
13. Psalm 130:1
14. Psalm 88:2-3
15. Psalm 55:1,4, 12-13
16. Psalm 55:17-18
17. R.S. Thomas, 'Emerging', *Collected Poems*, p.263
18. Sheila Upjohn, *All Shall be Well*, (Darton, Longman and Todd, 1992), p.82
19. Julian of Norwich, *Enfolded in Love*, p.23
20. Thomas Hardy, 'On the Departure Platform', *Collected Poems*, p.205
21. Harold Monro, 'Midnight Lamentation', *Poems of Today*, (Macmillan, 1945), p.116
22. Ibid., p.117
23. Lam. 3:44
24. Michael Hollings and Etta Gullick, *The One Who Listens*, (Mayhew-McCrimmon, 1971), p.146
25. Edith Forrest, 'Thanksgiving', *A Touch of Flame*, Ed. Jenny Robertson, (Lion, 1989), p.149

26. Edwin Muir, *Collected Poems*, p.227
27. Frances Cornford, 'The Quarrel', *Collected Poems*, (Cresset Press, 1954), p.103
28. Elizabeth Jennings, 'My Grandmother', *Collected Poems*, p.50
29. Julian of Norwich, *Enfolded in Love*, p.46, 52
30. Helen Waddell, 'Requiem for the Abbess of Gandesheim', *Lion Christian Poetry*, p.482

CHAPTER VI

Commonplace

Outside the open window
The morning air is all awash with angels
(Richard Wilbur)

The eyes open to a cry of pulleys,
And spirited from sleep, the astonished soul
Hangs for a moment bodiless and simple
As false dawn.
      Outside the open window
The morning air is all awash with angels.

    Some are in bed-sheets, some are in blouses,
Some are in smocks, but truly there they are.
Now they are rising together in calm swells
Of halcyon feeling, filling whatever they wear
With the deep joy of their impersonal breathing;

    Now they are flying in place, conveying
The terrible speed of their omnipresence, moving
And staying like white water; and now of a sudden
They swoon down into so rapt a quiet
That nobody seems to be there.
      The soul shrinks

    From all that it is about to remember,
From the punctual rape of every blessed day,
And cries,
      'Oh let there be nothing on earth but laundry,
Nothing but rosy hands in the rising steam
And clear dances done in the sight of heaven.'

Yet as the sun acknowledges
With a warm look the world's hunks and colours,
The soul descends once more in bitter love
To accept the waking body, saying now
In a changed voice as the man yawns and rises,
   'Bring them down from their ruddy gallows;
Let there be clean linen for the backs of thieves;
Let lovers go fresh and sweet to be undone,
And the heaviest nuns walk in a pure floating
Of dark habits,
      keeping their difficult balance.'[1]

Richard Wilbur calls this poem 'Love Calls us to the Things of This World', a title which can hold several meanings. One, I believe, is that the God who is love calls us to find something of his glory in the ordinariness of creation, to see him and to experience him in the everyday things of life, even such as washing on a line. To seek God in these things, to be open to the moments of transformation which the grace of God brings, is a form of prayer; it is to have God with us in all things, not pushed into some particular slot labelled 'prayer time'. Great men and women of prayer come down to our level when they find God in the commonplace; they may well tend to lose us when they enter the higher realms of contemplation of a vision of God that transports them out of this world. St Therese of Lisieux found Christ most abundantly present to her, not during hours of prayer (of which there were many) but rather in the midst of daily occupations. In the Benedictine Rule, as in other monastic rules, worship of God is centred upon and maintained by a regular cycle of three activities: corporate worship in the daily offices; study and meditation; and menial tasks and manual labour. Each is given its allotted time; each is significant and important, the menial no less than the others. A modern writer has said: 'St Benedict seeks God in the most simple and ordinary experiences.'[2] Benedict laid it down in his Rule that the cellarer 'will regard all the monastic utensils and goods of the monastery as if they were the sacred vessels'. To look for God in the routines and chores of everyday life, and to find him, must be an essential part of our growth in prayer.

> Only he who gives thanks for little things receives the big things. We prevent God from giving us the great spiritual gifts he has in store for us, because we do not give thanks for daily gifts. We think we dare not be satisfied with the small measure of spiritual knowledge, experience and love that has been given to us, and that we must constantly be looking forward eagerly for the highest good. Then we deplore the fact that we lack the deep certainty, the strong faith and the rich experience that God has given to others, and we consider this lament to be pious. We pray for the big things and forget to give thanks for the ordinary, small (and yet not really small) gifts. How can God entrust great things to one who will not thankfully receive from him the little things? If we do not give thanks daily for the Christian fellowship in which we have been placed, even where there is no great experience, no discoverable riches, but much weakness, small faith and difficulty; if on the contrary we only keep complaining to God that everything is so paltry and petty, so far from what we expected, then we hinder God from letting our fellowship grow according to the measure and riches which are there for us all in Jesus Christ.[3]

John Keble's hymn is a familiar statement of the necessity of finding God's grace in the commonplace:

> New every morning is the love
> Our waking and uprising prove;
> Through sleep and darkness safely brought
> Restored to life and power and thought.
>
> The trivial round, the common task,
> Will furnish all we ought to ask,
> Room to deny ourselves, a road
> To bring us daily nearer God.

And, we might note, the trivial round, the common task, should give us, not only room to deny ourselves, but room to fulfil ourselves. Yet, our prayers are, all too often, an attempt to escape from the trivial round and are a heartfelt request to get us through the day and into a bit of peace and quiet. We forget Keble's other lines in the same hymn:

> We need not bid for cloistered cell,
> Our neighbour and our work farewell.

One of the hardest battles in spiritual life, perhaps I should say the hardest, is the struggle to see God in trivial human happenings. How often we have to renew our act of faith! At first we are tempted to see only ourselves, to believe only in ourselves, to value only ourselves. Then gradually we perceive that the thread of life has a rationale, a mysterious unity, and we are led to think that we meet God in its basic stages. Then again, as our religious experience grows, we begin to realize that we meet God not only in the big events of our lives but in all events, however small and apparently insignificant. God is never absent from our lives. He cannot be, because 'in him we live and move, and have our being'. But it requires so much effort to turn this truth into a habit! We need repeated acts of faith before we learn to sail with confidence on the 'immense and endless sea' which is God, (St Gregory of Nazienzen) knowing that if we founder we do so in him, the divine, the eternal, the ever-present God.[4]

The God to whom we pray is one who makes himself known to us at our level. How else would we know him? This is not a matter of bringing God down to our level; it is a matter of recognizing a God who can speak to us even through the trivial to give us some perception of his glory, a glory that is seamless, yet perceived by us in fits and starts and with only partial glimpses. R.S. Thomas gives praise to the God of the big and of the little things, the God to whom we pray best in the simplicity of our yearning:

> I praise you because
> you are artist and scientist
> in one. When I am somewhat
> fearful of your power,
> your ability to work miracles

with a set-square, I hear
you murmuring to yourself
in a notation Beethoven
dreamed of but never achieved.
You run off your scales of
rain water and sea water, play
the chords of the morning
and evening light, sculpture
with shadow, join together leaf
by leaf, when spring
comes, the stanzas of
an immense poem. You speak
all languages and none,
answering our most complex
prayers with the simplicity
of a flower, confronting
us, when we would domesticate you
to our uses, with the rioting
viruses under our lens.[5]

How may we enrich and inform our prayer life by rooting part
of it in the commonplace? And how, if we do this, are we to avoid
the pitfall of becoming so attached to material or trivial things, to
everyday routines, that we are ruled by them? The short, and
difficult, answer to both questions is that we must learn to
commit these things to God in real thanksgiving for his grace and,
in so doing, we become more aware of God's presence in the
world in very ordinary things and events. We could start by
recognizing a paradox:

> We want life to have a meaning, we want fulfilment, healing and
> even ecstasy, but the human paradox is that we find these things by
> starting where we are, not where we wish we were. We must look
> for blessings to come from unlikely, everyday places – out of Galilee,
> as it were – and not in spectacular events, such as the coming of a
> comet.[6]

We must widen our concept of reverence so that we become

aware of the sacramental possibility in all things. It is here that the poet helps us and leads us on.

> The best poetic images, while they resonate with possibilities for transformation, are resolutely concrete, specific, incarnational. Concepts such as wonder or even holiness, are not talked about so much as presented for the reader's contemplation.[7]

Christianity is the most material of religions. The greatest reverence is given to those ordinary, everyday things of bread and wine. We believe that God came into the world to live as a man.

> The Bible is full of evidence that God's attention is indeed fixed on the little things. But this is not because God is a Great Cosmic Cop, eager to catch us in minor transgressions, but simply because God loves us – loves us so much that the divine presence is revealed even in the meaningless workings of daily life. It is in the ordinary, the here-and-now, that God asks us to recognize that the creation is indeed refreshed like dew-laden grass, that it is 'renewed in the morning' (Psalm 90:5), or, to put it in more personal and also theological terms, 'our inner nature is being renewed every day' (2 Cor. 4:16).[8]

Richard Wilbur's world is one of awareness of all the possibilities for revelation and renewal in this untidy, boisterous, violent world of ours. He calls us to thanksgiving, to openness to God. e.e. cummings beckons down the same path:

> i thank You God for this most amazing
> day: for the leaping greenly spirits of trees
> and a blue true dream of sky; and for everything
> which is natural which is infinite which is yes
>
> (i who have died am alive again today,
> and this is the sun's birthday; this is the birth
> day of life and of love and wings: and of the gay
> great happening illimitably earth)
>
> how should tasting touching hearing seeing
> breathing any – lifted from the no

of all nothing – human merely being
doubt unimaginable You?

(now the ears of my ears awake and
now the eyes of my eyes are opened)[9]

Thanksgiving here spills over, drunkenly almost, into the reward of faith grounded in the glory of God. The willingness to be open to God is rewarded by an awareness of him in 'everything which is natural.' Prayer becomes an experience in which 'ears are awake and eyes are opened.' Unlike cummings, Wilbur does not get lost in the sheer exuberance of wonder. In his poem there is a deep and tragic interplay between the purity of the morning and the stains of the world. Life is always a delicate and enormously difficult balance. With a warm and responsive look at the world's freshness and colours, the soul descends to the countless acts of love waiting to be done, needing to be done, in the face of rejection and apathy.

To pray for an opening of the eyes so that one may perceive something of the glory of God in the world is to seek a greater sensitivity to the world as it is, a mixture of glory and pain. William Blake saw the reflected glory of God in the ordinariness of things:

> To see the World in a grain of sand,
> And a Heaven in a wild flower,
> Hold Infinity in the palm of your hand,
> And Eternity in an hour.

He does not stay long in rapt contemplation, but is brought into the reality of the brokenness of the world:

> Man was made for Joy and Woe,
> And when this we rightly know
> Thro' the world we safely go.
> Joy and woe are woven fine,
> A clothing for the soul divine;
> Under every grief and pine
> Runs a joy with silken twine.[10]

To seek and to find God in the commonplace moves us far from the sort of coy sentimentality which Evelyn Underhill falls into in her poem Immanence:

> I come in the little things,
> Saith the Lord:
> Yea! on the glancing wings
> Of eager birds, the softly pattering feet
> Of furred and gentle beasts, I come to meet
> Your hard and wayward heart.[11]

I find Turgenev nearer the mark:

I saw myself in a dream, a youth, almost a boy, in a low-pitched, wooden church. The slim wax candles gleamed, spots of red before the old pictures of the saints. A ring of coloured light encircled every tiny flame. Dark and dim it was in the church . . . But there stood before me many people. All fair-haired, peasant heads. From time to time they began swaying, falling, rising again like the ripe ears of wheat when the wind of summer passes in slow undulation over them. All at once some man came up from behind me and stood beside me. I did not turn towards him; but at once felt that this man was Christ. Emotion, curiosity, awe overmastered me suddenly. I made an effort and looked at him. A face like every one's, a face like all men's faces. The eyes looked a little upwards, quietly and intently. The lips closed but not compressed; the upper lip, as it were, resting on the lower; a small beard, parted in two. The hands folded and still. And the clothes on him like everyone's. 'What sort of Christ is this?' I thought. 'Such an ordinary, ordinary man! It can't be!'

I turned away. But I had hardly turned my eyes away from this ordinary man when I felt again that it really was none other than Christ standing beside me. Again I made an effort over myself. And again the same face, like all men's faces, the same everyday though unknown features. And suddenly I came to myself. Only then I realised that just such a face – a face like all men's faces – is the face of Christ.[12]

Joan Rowbottom points out the agony which greater awareness brings. To seek prayer in the commonplace is to find, not only wonder and joy, it is to make continual intercession of directly experienced pain and distress. It is to recognize and accept the responsibility of shared pain:

> I have seen Christ
> in the neglected face of an unloved boy
>
> I have seen Christ
> in the gentleness and faith of an old man
>
> I have seen Christ
> in the quick hands of a nurse
> who knew I needed her before I asked
>
> I have seen Christ
> born again in spirit
> in the joyful song of a bright-faced child
>
> I have seen Christ
> when my heart was breaking
> in the compassionate eyes of a friend
>
> I have seen Christ
> in the forgiveness of a loved one
>
> I have seen Christ
> in the anguish of a mother for her dying son
>
> I have seen Christ
> in a dustman and a doctor
>
> God grant
> that they may see Christ in me.[13]

The ordinariness of Christ is a contradiction in terms, part of the paradox we constantly face as we try to come to terms with the experience of God's grace in our lives. It is the same paradox we face in our prayers as we bring ourselves in all our littleness before the greatness of an all-loving God. To be brought close to Christ is to be given wonder and joy in the timeless world of the spirit and it is also to be rooted in the demands of relationships, even the chance encounter with a stranger:

One of the crowd went up,
And knelt before the Paten and the Cup,
Received the Lord, returned in peace, and prayed
Close by my side. Then in my heart I said:

O Christ, in this man's life –
This stranger who is Thine – in all his strife,
All his felicity, his good and ill,
In the assaulted stronghold of his will,

I do confess Thee here
Alive within this life; I know Thee near
Within this lonely conscience, closed away,
Within this brother's solitary day,

Christ in his unknown heart,
His intellect unknown – this love, this art,
This battle and this peace, this destiny
That I shall never know, look upon me!

Christ in his numbered breath,
Christ in his beating heart and in his death,
Christ in his mystery! From that secret place
And from that separate dwelling, give me grace.[14]

Alan Ecclestone, in commenting upon this poem says: 'On
retiring to Gosforth and going to church, I knelt among people
who as yet were anonymous. Yet each person there required of me
that I say the second stanza of this poem. It is so easy to half-
acknowledge and not to notice that the Christ is in them. It is
humbling too for the one who has presided at the Holy
Communion to look out at the people on leaving the altar, to
look on Christ embodied. In which direction should one bow?'[15]
To see a person as God-given, whatever their form or circum-
stance, is prayer. We are humbled by such knowledge and made
more aware of our dependence upon others and upon God. To be
made more aware of the God-given humanity of another person,
even in a chance encounter, is a gift of grace and it is often hard
to bear. For to experience deeply the vulnerability of another

person is to expose our own vulnerability, our own powerlessness. Such experiences are hard to live with and would reduce us to helplessness were it not for the contrary awareness granted to us of aspects of the resurrection, of the power of rejuvenating life. These things, too, come to us through the commonplace.

> As sure as what is most sure, sure as that spring primroses
> Shall new-dapple next year, sure as tomorrow morning,
> Amongst come-back-again things, things with a revival, things with
> a recovery,
> Thy name . . .[16]

To have that sudden perception of overwhelming hope, however dimly perceived (and even Hopkins in his poem tails off into an inarticulate 'Thy name') is to know the resurrection, **now**. That surge of hope gives new life to our prayers, to our whole being.

The stupendous reality of the resurrection now is not to be grasped through intellectual constructions, nor through theological debate, but through the grace of God granting us a perception of the truth. And that grace is offered to us very often through the transformation of the ordinariness of things. We should not be surprised by this. The new-found confidence and joy of the previously demoralized and shattered followers of Jesus came from the homely reality of a risen Lord who ate breakfast with them, who could talk about fishing, who walked a country road, who was mistaken for a gardener. The resurrection has to do with hope and newness now, as well as with a hope for a future life that we cannot conceive of.

> We are to pray, no matter how hidden the inmost room from which it is made, as those who are, up to their full capacity, to grow in wonder and delight at the vast context of God's action. We are to pray, no matter how still our bodies, as those who are sustained by the great tidal wave of his oncoming Kingdom. We are to pray, no matter how silent our lips, as those who join the dawn-chorus of a new creation.[17]

As we offer intercession to God for those things that trouble and concern us, we ask him for the gift of hope. And we are given hope in so many different ways. Sometimes hope comes as we see our prayers being answered. But prayers are rarely answered as we would wish them to be. This is when we need the hope that is an assurance of God being with us, sharing the burdens, giving us strength and courage to carry on. That hope comes to us, so very often, in the lifting of the heart, sudden and momentary perhaps, but real enough and potent in its assurance, a touch of joy from the transformation of a very ordinary and otherwise insignificant thing. To be open to God through the routine ordinariness of things and events and encounters is prayer. The resurrection **now** comes in small things, reassuringly and hopefully. The hope we are granted in such moments of transformation should be offered back to God in thanksgiving.

Poets are sensitive to moments of transformation; they share their perceptions with us, the reader, to make of them what we will. Theirs is the gift, also, of being able to see through the eyes of others, enabling them to enter worlds closed to us or but dimly perceived. Sometimes, they may offer us joy and hope which come from the infinite possibilities of the world seen through the eyes of a child:

> When we climbed the slopes of the cutting
> We were eye-level with the white cups
> Of the telegraph poles and the sizzling wires.
>
> Like lovely freehand they curved for miles
> East and miles west beyond us, sagging
> Under their burden of swallows.
>
> We were small and thought we knew nothing
> Worth knowing. We thought words travelled the wires
> In the shiny pouches of raindrops,
> Each one seeded with the light
>
> Of the sky, the gleam of the lines, and ourselves
> So infinitesimally scaled
>
> We could stream through the eye of a needle.[18]

Our prayers are crabbed and restricted by thinking we know nothing worth knowing, by limiting God to the confines of our little world, by thinking that his glory is sparingly given. To pray for hope is to pray that our eyes will be opened to new perceptions that will spring out to us from something as ordinary as a telephone wire in the rain.

A prayer of St Leo is one that I find both helpful and challenging: 'O God you created man most wonderfully, but still more wonderfully renewed him; grant that we may become sharers in his divine nature, who has deigned to share our human nature.' It is an audacious request to God, and yet one we must not be afraid to make. To seek to become sharers in the divine nature of Christ is not, as I see it, asking to be transported into another world of the spirit, but is asking to know the risen, contemporary Christ in the world as it is. It is to ask for the risen Lord to come to us where we are and, in so doing, to make himself known to us in renewals of the spirit in everyday encounters. To grasp a moment of wonder from something as common and untidy as a weed is to be given a prayer that will illuminate a day:

> They won't let railways alone those yellow flowers.
> They're that remorseless joy of dereliction
> darkest banks exhale like vivid breath
> as bricks divide to let them root between.
> How every falling place concocts their smile,
> taking what's left and making a song of it.[19]

Here is what we might call casual holiness, seen even in ragwort, but no less moving and wonderful for that. To catch some note of glory in the mundane ordinariness of life is not a cheapening of the majesty of God, not if it brings renewal, not if it breaks through the routines that keep us enclosed in a world that would exclude him. If the poet helps us to see something of a sacrament as men in allotments go about their work, that is not fanciful imagination; it is a true perception of a world which can enter our prayers and bring us close to God:

As mute as monks, tidy as bachelors,
They manicure their little plots of earth.
Pop music from the council estate
Counterpoints with the Sunday morning bells,
But neither siren voice has power for these
Drab solitary men who spend their time
Kneeling, or fetching water, soberly,
Or walking softly down a row of beans.

Like drill sergeants, they measure their recruits.
The infant sprig receives the proper space
The manly full grown cauliflower will need.
And all must toe the line here; stem and leaf,
As well as root, obey the rule of string.
Domesticated tilth aligns itself
In sweet conformity but head in air
Soars the unruly loveliness of beans.

They visit the hidden places of the earth
When tenderly with fork and hand they grope
To lift potatoes, and the round, flushed globes
Tumble like pearls out of the moving soil.
They share their strange intuitions, know how much
Patience and energy and sense of poise
It takes to be an onion; and they share
The subtle benediction of the beans.

They see the casual holiness that spreads
Along obedient furrows. Cabbages
Unfurl their veined and rounded fans in joy,
And buds of sprouts rejoice along their stalks.
The ferny tops of carrots, stout red stems
Of beetroot, zany sunflowers with blond hair
And bloodshot faces, shine like seraphim
Under the long flat fingers of the beans.[20]

Laborare est orare; work is prayer; we are told. Does that include men on allotments? It would be easier to accept that than the repetitive actions on a production line or the operation of a supermarket till. In talking of work as prayer, we are more likely to be thinking of something we call creative, something with some personal commitment to the outcome. To see a finished work of art or craftsmanship is indeed to see the outcome of prayer as work, in which the artist or craftsman is humbled before the creative process, in which the finished work becomes an offering, containing something of the spirit of the creator.

> This Chinese bowl
> is barely tangible,
> thin-skinned
> as if spun from light.
>
> Poised between
> form and disintegration,
> it almost breaks
> at the edge of vision;
>
> a taut perfection.
>
> We whisper
> lest our voices turn
> it to dust,
> know tenderness at
> the passion of its survival.
>
> It is the tremor
> we feel when children
> in cardboard crowns
> tell the Christmas story.
>
> this is our faith;
> worked clay defeating death.[21]

To be able to create something that will last is beyond most of us. We cannot get anywhere near an achievement of 'worked clay defeating death'. Our efforts go into ephemeral things. Yet I doubt very much whether the person of great creative ability is thinking of posterity when they produce their work of lasting quality. What matters to them, the prayerful aspect of it, is that they give something of themselves. It is when we stop giving of ourselves in the everyday tasks that make up so much of our lives, when we just want to get these things out of the way so that we can 'enjoy the things that matter', that routines become chores and burdens, so very far removed from anything to do with prayer, except that we may pray to have done with them.

It is a paradox of human life that in worship, as in human love, it is in the routine and the everyday that we find the possibilities for the greatest transformation. Both worship and housework often seem perfunctory. And both, by the grace of God, may be anything but. At its Latin root, *perfunctory* means 'to get through with', and we can easily see how liturgy, laundry and what has been traditionally conceived of as 'women's work' can be done in that indifferent spirit. But the joke is on us: what we think we are only 'getting through' has the power to change us, just as we have the power to transform what seems meaningless – the endless repetitions of a litany or the motions of vacuuming a floor. What we dread as mindless activity can free us, mind and heart, for the workings of the Holy Spirit, and the repetitive motions are conducive to devotions such as the Jesus Prayer or the Rosary. Anything is fair game for prayer, anything or anyone who pops into the mind can be included.[22]

'Anything is fair game for prayer', and we need to bring our great thoughts, our flights of reverence and awe, back to the everyday world which both nourishes us and takes so much out of us. Ursula Fanthorpe's poem 'Atlas' has not an ounce of romantic love in it, yet presents us with the aspect of love which keeps us going, not as rare moments of delight or wonder, but as day in, day out, maintenance. This is the love which 'bears all things, endures all things.' But, unlike Paul's paragon, it may well be, at times, impatient and irritable, but it will never end. So, too, our prayers.

> There is a kind of love called maintenance,
> Which stores the WD40 and knows when to use it;
>
> Which checks the insurance, and doesn't forget
> The milkman, which remembers to plant bulbs;

Which answers letters, which knows the way
The money goes, which deals with dentists

And Road Fund Tax and meeting trains,
And postcards to the lonely, which upholds
The permanently rickety elaborate
Structures of living; which is Atlas.

And maintenance is the sensible kind of love,
Which knows what time and weather are doing
To my brickwork; insulates my faulty wiring;
Laughs at my dry-rotten jokes, remembers
My need for gloss and grouting; which keeps
My suspect edifice upright in the air,
As Atlas did the sky.[23]

Sources

1. Richard Wilbur, 'Love Calls us to the Things of This World', *New and Collected Poems*, (Faber and Faber, 1988), p.233
2. Esther de Waal, *Seeking God*, (Fount, 1984), p.99
3. Dietrich Bonhoeffer, *Life Together*, (SCM, 1963), p.19
4. Carlo Caretto, *Love is for Loving*, (Darton, Longman and Todd, 1976), p.109
5. R.S. Thomas, 'Praise', *Collected Poems*, p.318
6. Kathleen Norris, *The Quotidian Mysteries*, (Paulist Press, 1998), p.12
7. Ibid., p.12
8. Ibid., p.21
9. e.e. cummings, *Selected Poems*, p.76
10. William Blake, 'Auguries of Innocence', *Oxford Book of Nineteenth Century English Verse*, (Oxford, 1964), p.28
11. Evelyn Underhill, *Immanence*, (J.M. Dent, undated), p.1
12. Ivan Turgenev, *Dream Tales and Prose Poems, A Treasury of the Kingdom*, (Oxford, 1954), p.266
13. Joan Rowbottom in *A Touch of Flame*, complied by Jenny Roberts, (Lion, 1989), p.32

14. Alice Meynell, 'The Unknown God', *Prose and Poetry* (Jonathan Cape, 1947), p.372
15. Alan Ecclestone, *Gather the Fragments*, (Cairns Publications, 1993), p.11
16. G.M. Hopkins, 'St Winefred's Well', *The Poems of Gerard Manley Hopkins*, p.193
17. Alan Ecclestone, *Yes to God*, p.125
18. Seamus Heaney, 'The Railway Children', *New and Collected Poems 1966-1987*, (Faber and Faber, 1990), p.159
19. Anne Stevenson, 'Ragwort', *The Collected Poems*, (Oxford, 1966), p.61
20. U.A. Fanthorpe, 'Men on Allotments', *Selected Poems*, (Penguin, 1986), p.31
21. Isobel Thrilling, 'Creation', *The Lion Christian Poetry Collection*, p.194
22. Kathleen Norris, op. cit., p.82
23. U.A. Fanthorpe, 'Atlas', *Safe as Houses*, (Peterloo Poets, 1995)

Index of Authors